CONTINUING

PROFESSIONAL

DEVELOPMENT

CONTINUING

PROFESSIONAL

DEVELOPMENT

PERSPECTIVES ON CPD IN PRACTICE

EDITED BY
SANDRA CLYNE

**KOGAN
PAGE**

Dedication

This book is dedicated to my husband, Dr Kenn Hodd. His support, generosity, wisdom and unfailing encouragement never cease to astound and delight me.

First published in 1995

Apart from any fair dealing for the purposes of research or private study, or criticism or review, as permitted under the Copyright, Designs and Patents Act, 1988, this publication may only be reproduced, stored or transmitted, in any form or by any means, with the prior permission in writing of the publishers, or in the case of reprographic reproduction in accordance with the terms of licences issued by the Copyright Licensing Agency. Enquiries concerning reproduction outside those terms should be sent to the publishers at the undermentioned address:

Kogan Page Limited
120 Pentonville Road
London N1 9JN

© Sandra Clyne and named contributors, 1995

British Library Cataloguing in Publication Data

A CIP record for this book is available from the British Library.

ISBN 0 7494 1253 4

Typeset by Saxon Graphics Ltd, Derby
Printed and bound in Great Britain by Biddles Ltd, Guildford and Kings Lynn.

Contents

Acknowledgements

The editor would like to thank the writers for their stimulating and exciting contributions, and all the professionals who gave generously of their time to participate in the research which is reported in Chapter 15.

The editor is grateful to all the people who helped to find solutions to problems, particularly related to computing; to the CPD networks and contacts for opening many doors to new ideas; to friends and 'the girls', Suzanne, Nina and Daisy, for their endless good humour and patience.

And finally, to Kogan Page and their editorial staff, who provided the opportunity to create the book.

About the Contributors

Christopher Bond is a graduate in Theology from Westminster College Oxford. He spent his early career as an educational adviser to a number of health care professional bodies. From this he generated an interest in CPD for health professionals and worked as the Education and Training Officer for the British Dietetic Association.

He left this post to take up a Senior Lecturer post at the University of Central England Business School. He teaches management learning and organizational behaviour, is Course Director for an undergraduate degree and manages the Credit Accumulation and Transfer Unit and Accreditation of Prior Learning centre.

He has acted as consultant to a number of organizations and specializes in HR and OD-related activity. He has published widely in the training field on flexible approaches to learning and development.

Sandra Clyne has worked primarily in the area of adult vocational development. She has carried out research into the training and development needs of women managers, has been a university lecturer and assistant director of the management programme at Brunel University. She has also worked at British Telecom as an internal consultant.

Currently, she works as an independent consultant concentrating on CPD, coaching and career development.

Heather Crockett is project officer in the Department of Continuing Education at Lancaster University and is responsible for much of the work described in Chapter 10.

She has previously worked with entrepreneurs – many of them 'lone professionals' – in leisure and tourism. She has run her own businesses and been involved in a number of development initiatives in vocational education.

Carol Dix, former *Guardian* journalist and author of many books, now works as a press and PR consultant for South Bank University, London, and as a consultant editor and writer of brochures, company reports and documents.

She has worked on several major projects for the Local Government Management Board, including manual worker training developments, graduate recruitment and continuous professional development.

Lynn Drury, Cheltenham Strategic Publications, is an independent researcher, editor and writer specializing in reports on management and information technology issues and the design of distance learning and technology-based training materials. She is co-author of two recent books on the future of the professions: *From Evolution to Revolution: The Pressure of Professional Life in the 1990s*, and *Positioning for the Unknown: Career Development for Professionals in the 1990s*. She is currently involved in preparing good practice guides and distance learning packs on research supervision and on career development issues for professionals.

John Geale, a Senior Research Fellow in the Department of Continuing Education at Lancaster, has 35 years experience of industry and higher education. Much of the time has been spent where the two meet: technology transfer, careers and continuing education.

He has worked for a number of government departments/agencies on professional updating initiatives and was Director of Continuing Education at Bradford University from 1985 to 1990.

Andrew Gibbons is a Fellow of the Institute of Personnel and Development, and a member of their continuous professional development working party. He holds Diplomas in Personnel Management and Training Management. Currently, he is an independent consultant and has a particular interest in helping people to learn and in the development of long-term sustainable changes.

He has an enduring interest in assisting professional bodies with CPD. He facilitates 'learning from work' events, writes extensively on self-managed learning and related aspects of CPD.

Anna Hughes has worked for universities, the voluntary sector and the European Parliament, bringing this experience together in the publication *Developing European Professions: Delivering Continuing Professional Development in Europe* (1994).

Most of Anna's work experience has been in public relations

and training for large not-for-profit and public organizations. Her experience of the continental European workplace, and the field-work for the report named above, have given her a wide insight into European continuing development systems.

Anna is currently employed by the Graduate School for International Business at Bristol University.

Nigel Hughes was educated at Highgate School and the University of East Anglia and trained as a Chartered Accountant with Deloitte Haskins and Sells.

Following posts in various accountancy firms which combined training and practice work he formed his own company which provides training and consultancy in both financial and management areas. Originally established to devise and deliver high quality training programmes to the accountancy profession, its services have expanded to include training for lawyers, new businesses and companies abroad.

He is also closely involved with the development and maintenance of standards for a number of accounting institutes as well as being external examiner for Oxford Brookes University.

Paul Kalinauckas is Joint Managing Director of the Escatel Group, a team of consultants who specialize in bringing coaching-based solutions to all types of business issues. He acted as the subject expert for the BBC video on Coaching for Results and was commissioned by the Institute of Personnel and Development to write a book on *Coaching – Realising the Potential*. He has worked as a professional coach in a wide variety of organizations with individuals committed to improving personal performance. He is a visiting lecturer at Oxford University and the University of Warwick.

Prior to setting up as a coach he was Secretary General of the British Junior Chamber of Commerce and then worked for a leading European training and development company on productivity improvement, customer service and quality.

John Lorriman has international experience as a training consultant, public speaker and writer. He is the author of The Engineering Council's *Continuing Professional Development – The practical guide to good practice* and has followed this up by editing a thrice-yearly CPD newsletter – *CPD Link* – for The Engineering Council.

He was for several years responsible for training, internal communications and manpower planning for GEC's telecommunications business as well as editing GEC's corporate training newsletter.

He is chairman of the professional working group of the International Association for Continuing Engineering Education (the world umbrella body for CEE) and is also a member of the BTEC Engineering Advisory Board and an executive member of the Cambridge University Engineering Association.

Dennis Neale started his business life as a pupil architect and studied architecture at the Regent Street Polytechnic. From 1939 to 1944 he served in the infantry, mainly in the Middle East. After the war, he returned to architecture and was later a planning officer in a local authority. After a brief spell with the British Standards Institution he joined the Institute of Builders – now the Chartered Institute of Building – as Chief Executive in 1955. During his 30 years' service the Institute developed as a major institution for building professionals.

He retired at the end of 1985 and took up the post of Secretary of the Education and Training Committee of the Construction Industry Council. He was appointed OBE in 1971 for services to building and the Institute. He is an Honorary Fellow of the Institute and of the American Institute of Constructors.

Clare Rapkins (née Madden) was Staff Tutor in Professional Practice Management for Continuing Education in the Department for Continuing Education at Bristol University.

She is the author of *Professions, Standards and Competence: A survey of continuing education for the professions* (1993). Her specialist experience is in the field of occupational psychology, particularly professional development and recruitment.

Clare is currently employed by the Chartered Institute of Public Finance and Accountancy (CIPFA) as post qualification development manager, where she is responsible for the development of policy and practice for continuing professional development.

Christopher Senior underwent initial training and job experience as a design/commissioning engineer and he has over 20 years experience in training and development including work with Babcock Engineering, Balfour Beatty, Manpower Services Commission and the Department of Education and Science.

Since 1988 he has been employed at the Engineering Council as senior executive responsible for setting standards and promoting the action on continuing professional development throughout the engineering profession. He has carried out studies of CPD across a number of professions, led national and international projects on professional development for engineers and established standards for CPD.

Graham Taylor joined British Rail as a mechanical craft apprentice with Southern Railway and progressed to technical training and supervisory posts. When the Industrial Training Boards were created he became responsible for the development and implementation of Standard-based Training for Craft Apprentices. Later, as works training officer, he was responsible for the training of all categories of staff including supervisory and management at the Eastleigh Works.

He then took on a group appontment as training adviser to the HQ personnel manager responsible for coordinating and developing training over the company's six sites and HQ. Eventually, he left Eastleigh and became group training and development manager at the company's HQ at Derby.

Sandra Tjok-a-Tam has had extensive experience in the personnel and management development fields in public and manufacturing sectors. She was a personnel manager for manufacturing organizations and a tutor and course director for postgraduate management programmes at Croydon College. Sandra established and managed, in 1991, one of the first MCI Management Centres and was responsible for the design and delivery of management NVQ programmes.

Sandra obtained a PhD that specifically focused upon the areas of management learning; management development and organizational change and related use of the management standards, NVQs and APL processes. Her special business interest focuses upon the growth of access to learning opportunities for managers and organizational learning programmes. She established in early 1994 a Management Consultancy, Qudos South East, whose business aim is to: 'Improve Business Performance Through the Development of People'.

Jeff Watkins is Continuing Professional Development Coordinator at the University of Bristol. He has published extensively in the area of professional development and information management and is currently course leader on the modular masters degree in management which has been specially devised for professionals. He has recently carried out two major research surveys on the key changes currently affecting the professional workforce and on the changing career patterns of professional people. The results of the first survey were published in 1992 in the book *From Evolution to Revolution: The Pressure of Professional Life in the 1990s*, and the results of the second were published in *Positioning for the Unknown: Career Development for Professionals in the 1990s*. His latest publication is *Managing the Transition: A Comprehensive Study of the Changing Use of IT in the Retail Financial Services Sector*.

Introduction

Sandra Clyne

THE FOCUS OF THE BOOK

What the book is about

This book is about Continuing Professional Development (also known as Continuing or Continuous Professional Education). Whichever term is used the message is the same: it's the way in which professionals keep themselves up-to-date and maintain their standards as professionals in the practice of the work that they do.

Definitions vary, but one which is commonly accepted and is used elsewhere in this volume is the one adopted by the inter-professional CPD in Construction Group:

> The systematic maintenance, improvement and broadening of knowledge and skill and the development of personal qualities necessary for the execution of professional and technical duties throughout the practitioner's working life.

A further definition is provided by Cyril Houle (1980):

> The ways in which professionals try, throughout their active lives of service, to refresh their own knowledge and ability and build a sense of collective responsibility to society.

This definition stretches the responsibility of the professional beyond their personal development and recognizes that professionals have a special responsibility and, by implication, a particular status in society. In order to maintain this status the professional is required to move beyond the achievement of initial qualification to CPD. Welsh and Woodward (1989) consider that the 'key issue is *competence*' and that, 'it is by CPD that individual professional competence is maintained and approved'. They also consider that the role of the professional bodies is not only about safeguarding standards but also about continuing competence and questions of CPD policy and practices. CPD is not a fringe activity: indeed, Todd (1987) considers it to be 'one of the most important resources a professional can draw on to maintain competence'.

Typically, CPD has been the the province of professionals who are members of established, traditional professional bodies. However, for the purpose of this book this definition has been extended to include 'new' professionals, many of whom are operating in areas of work that did not exist 30 years ago, and other professionals who are staking a claim for recognition although they may not have had the high status of, for example, accountants and doctors. The changing definition of 'professional' is addressed both explicitly and implicitly in various contributions.

So if this is the subject, who is being addressed? Who is this book for? Essentially, everyone who is involved in CPD, whether as a user, involved in the employment of professional staff, or as a provider of support.

Who is involved in CPD?

Using a term common in management development and HRD (Human Resource Development), who are the *stakeholders* in CPD? They include:

- the individual professional
- their employer, or partners in a practice
- their manager
- staff who are managed
- professional bodies
- providers
- clients
- government.

Those for whom this book will be most directly relevant are the individual, the professional bodies, the employer and providers. In addition, the HRD professional has a key role in managing the interface between the employer and individual professional. The book is intended for *anyone* interested in CPD and stresses the importance of *managing* development rather than treating it as an *ad hoc* activity.

For the *individual*, it is imperative that they both maintain their current level of competence and also keep up-to-date with changes. In broad terms there are three common reasons for professionals to engage in CPD; these are to:

- update themselves in new knowledge
- train themselves for additional roles demanded of them
- improve personal effectiveness (Vaughan, 1991).

It is no longer possible to practise the same things in the same way for the whole of your working life. Even if you stay within your specialism you will almost certainly find that your role changes. You may begin as an engineer but end up running a company or, more likely, becoming a manager. Your initial qualification gives you the start – CPD gives you the power to choose and change direction.

The period of initial training fits you to practise. When you have gained experience the picture changes and what you need is conscious learning from a variety of sources – hence the demand for both structured and unstructured learning experiences which constitute the most effective approaches to CPD.

The *professional bodies* are an essential element in traditional CPD. They have several roles including initial professional education and CPD; other aspects of their activities are examined within the book. The bodies vary in size of membership from a few hundred to over a hundred thousand. Some related professions cluster to form larger groupings which may give access to broader CPD provision – a kind of economy of scale which also enables smaller bodies to influence CPD policy and practice.

Professional bodies play a range of roles in relation to CPD. One of these is to safeguard standards so that the public has confidence in the maintenance of competence. 'Managing' CPD usually means creating a CPD scheme and underpinning this with support; it may also include monitoring compliance, although this is frequently a contentious issue.

The third partner in the CPD process is the *employer*. They have a responsibility to their clients to provide a competent and efficient professional service. The employer may have an appraisal and performance review system which is linked to the requirements of the professional body. Ideally, CPD should be a shared responsibility and partnership which results in the enhancement of the professional's competence. The employer needs to integrate the job-related competence required with what the professional body expects.

The final partner is the *provider* of courses and conferences. This is a specialist role which is provided by the body itself or a nominated and approved alternative. The idea that a 'provider' is always needed for CPD will not be favoured by those who regard

CPD as an opportunity for the individual to take ownership of their own learning. Nevertheless, for the moment at least, course provision is likely to be the mainstay of CPD. Of the other stakeholders, government currently has a largely 'hands-off' position, taking the view that CPD should be self-financing. Of the remaining stakeholders the position of the client is implicitly addressed as the beneficiary of CPD and the managers will support professionals in their CPD.

BACKGROUND TO THE BOOK

The need for the book

When I held the post of Learning Development Manager with the Institute of Training and Development (now combined with the Institute of Personnel Management to form the Institute of Personnel and Development) I was responsible for helping to develop and implement the Institute's CPD policy. Through this work I came into contact with a number of CPD specialists from a range of professional bodies and employment sectors. A number of us combined to create a group we called the 'CPD Forum' or 'CPD Network Group' to exchange ideas and information. This group is similar to the Inter-Professional Group whose most recent survey forms the Appendix to this volume). We identified some of the key questions which seemed to recur and to be important to many of us and to other colleagues involved in CPD. The issues raised included:

- monitoring participation in CPD – is it possible? Is it desirable?
- how standards are enforced – should they be? Is it possible?
- participation in CPD – mandatory or voluntary?
- who 'owns' CPD?
- how learners are supported
- the role of the employer and how CPD relates to employers' HRD practices
- maintenance of CPD during a career break
- how CPD is recorded and to what end
- how self-employed professionals maintain their CPD
- sources of information about CPD
- what counts as CPD
- who should provide CPD and how standards of provision are monitored.

I also started to receive queries from bemused managers who had 'just been made responsible for CPD' but didn't really know anything about it.

From this, it was clear that there was a need for a book which began to describe and examine some aspects of current practice, questions, ideas, new developments and approaches – to map the territory to show where 'there be dragons', where others have gone before and laid safe trails and paths and where brave souls are struggling towards solutions.

The world of CPD and of professionals is changing. A number of chapters in the book address these changes and their impact upon both theory and practice. For example, at one level, the development of information technology (IT) produces a new professional – the IT specialist who might, in time, have his or her own professional body. At another level, the current growth of IT affects most professionals inasmuch as they need to acquire IT skills – a whole new CPD area.

'Managing' CPD

The process of actively managing CPD gives the book a particular perspective as this emphasizes the need to recognize that CPD:

is not a destination but a lifelong process in which professionals engage;

has to be addressed consciously with awareness in order to recognize *what* it is and *how* it can be done;

is not a solitary activity carried out by an individual professional without reference to others, although it may sometimes feel that way.

There are many who have a legitimate vested interest in the success of an individual's CPD, as the earlier list of stakeholders demonstrates.

'Management' is often regarded in a narrow sense as the concern of major employers who have 'managers' who carry out a mysterious activity called 'managing'. In the context of CPD, managing is carried out by all stakeholders taking responsibility for the success of their part of the CPD process. The 'success' of an individual's CPD can be defined in many ways: it might be by fulfilling the minimum level of CPD activity required by the professional body or not falling asleep too conspicuously at courses.

It might be filling in your CPD record the night before it's called in or, more profitably by planning and measuring your CPD as part of your personal and professional development. All these are how CPD is done. At best, it is managed by all the stakeholders in the interest of improving the professional service provided.

THE CONTENT OF THE BOOK

When planning this book I quickly became aware of two factors that would strongly influence the content. These were that it would be impossible to cover every aspect of current CPD in a single volume and that most of the information about CPD was not widely published and available to be researched. This meant that the book had to be based partly upon published material but mainly upon the testimony of experts in the field who had been working or are currently working in the area.

I decided to commission chapters which reflect the priorities and questions which seem to concern the CPD community, as well as new approaches and developments. I also carried out a small research study of individuals' professional development which is presented in Chapter 15. Together this approach provides a variety of perspectives on CPD as it is currently practised.

The book is organized in two sections: the first, which I have called 'Institutions', focuses upon the professional bodies and some key industrial sectors; the second deals with 'Individuals' and their differing ways of managing CPD. Both sections are preceded by a brief introduction to the themes and ideas described and explored in that section. The book ends with a summary of significant points and a consideration of possible future developments and directions.

The chapters range in style from the intensely practical to the academic. However, they all stem from a recognition that there are profound changes taking place in the world of work and that professional practice has to meet these challenges if the professionals are to keep their role and status as an important and influential group.

REFERENCES

Houle, C (1980) *Continuing Learning in the Professions*, Jossey-Bass, San Francisco, CA.

Todd, F (1987) *Planning Continuing Professional Development*, Croom Helm, Beckenham, England.

Vaughan, P (1991) *Maintaining Professional Competence*, Department of Adult Education, University of Hull.

Welsh, L and Woodward, P (1989) *Continuing Professional Development: Towards a national strategy*, FE Unit (PICKUP), London and Glasgow.

Part One

INSTITUTIONS

Introduction to Part One

The first part of this book looks at professional bodies and particular occupational groups and sectors. Some general examination of trends is combined with specific examples of CPD in practice. The current context in which CPD operates and some of the questions and issues being discussed are included as well as trends and developments.

The book opens with a chapter by Jeff Watkins and Lynn Drury which is drawn from the extensive research carried out at Bristol University on the changing role of the professional. They look at the growth of the professional classes and the pressures on them to respond positively to these changes. This chapter sets out the agenda for the whole book: the rapid pace of change and the place of CPD in managing these changes.

The second chapter is provided by Dennis Neale who has had a long and distinguished career in the construction industry, most recently as co-ordinator of the CPD in Construction Group. He outlines the development of the Group, some of its achievements and the state of CPD in the professions and institutions in the construction industry. He also addresses some of the questions currently being discussed in the CPD community, including monitoring and record keeping, and draws some conclusions about professional competence.

In the third chapter, professional bodies and CPD are examined by Clare Rapkins whose material is drawn from the research she carried out at Bristol University. Two models of CPD policy and practice are presented and three case studies of good practice outlined. The chapter concludes with some recommendations for creating effective CPD schemes.

This is followed by Nigel Hughes' chapter in which he poses some searching questions about the effectiveness of traditional CPD schemes and focuses upon problems of compliance and relevance. He uses the experience of his own professional body of chartered accountants to illustrate the points he makes. He draws some lessons from this and suggests an alternative approach.

In Chapter Five, Chris Senior, CPD Executive at the Engineering Council, outlines some of the national and global changes that are making CPD increasingly important for engineers. The engineering industry has a long tradition of CPD and Chris examines some recent and current initiatives. He also identifies some of the issues such as motivation, commitment and support that are critical for successful CPD.

Chapter 6 outlines the CPD scheme created by British Rail in recognition of the need to respond positively to changes in the industry. Graham Taylor, British Rail's training and development manager, describes the process of design, implementation and review which was employed and highlights important issues raised by the project and lessons learnt.

In the next chapter, Anna Hughes writes about CPD in continental Europe. She outlines some of the similarities and differences in the legal position of CPD in six European countries and the contrasting approaches adopted by professional bodies. She also includes some case studies of CPD in Denmark, Germany and France.

The final chapter in this section is by Carol Dix whose work with the Local Government Management Board (LGMB) forms the basis for this chapter. She looks at the changing role of the professional and identifies some aspects of the new professionalism required in local government. She also identifies the need for partnerships beween employers, professional bodies and individuals and touches on the new developments of NVQs. She ends her chapter with questions about the way forward and pointers for further action.

1

The Professions in the 1990s

Jeff Watkins and Lynn Drury

This chapter, which begins by briefly examining the growth of professional classes in the UK, considers the major pressures or trends which will affect their roles over the next five years. Unless today's professional responds pro-actively to these pressures, the potential of their contribution to the economic success of the nation over the next decade will be wasted.

GROWTH OF THE PROFESSIONAL CLASSES

From an historical viewpoint we see the ranks of the traditional professions growing in numbers and the emergence of new professions through a process of specialization or in response to changes in the nature of commerce, the values of society and advances in technology (Watkins *et al.*, 1992). Today five groups of professionals can be distinguished by origin:

- post-industrial – knowledge workers
- enterprise – business, management specialists
- welfare – teachers, social workers
- industrial – engineers, chemists, accountants
- pre-industrial – lawyers, clergy, doctors.

The pre-industrial professions: divinity, medicine and law, which claimed expertise in the overriding concerns of early society – the soul, health and justice – were well established by the 18th century. Being backed by Charter from early times, they represent the most powerful groups today. The industrial era saw the growth of professions with the kind of expertise which transformed the economy from agricultural to industrial – the civil and mechanical engineer, the industrial chemist, the accountant and the banker. The birth of the 'welfare state' in the mid-20th

27

century saw the emergence of the welfare professions, and the latter half of the century, with its re-emphasis on the values of the market economy, saw the rise of the enterprise or management professions. As we approach the 21st century with its new emphasis on information, communications and the media, we see the emergence of new professionals in areas such as broadcasting, public relations and information technology. Information technology alone has a whole range of new professions – the knowledge engineer, software documenter, network designer, information broker.

Today the term 'professional' is used to describe the activities of a wide range of people across many occupational groups. The current Standard Occupational Classification defines a professional as one who has a degree and a postgraduate professional qualification. It lists nine major occupational groups. Major Group 2 identifies the main professional groups; in Major Group 1, which identifies managerial and administrative occupations, Minor Groups 12 and 13 are also generally regarded as professional occupations (see Table 1.1).

Professionals defined thus represent approximately 15 per cent of the workforce today and this is expected to reach 30 per cent

Table 1.1 *Standard occupational classifications (Wilson, 1991)*

MAJOR GROUP 2: PROFESSIONALS

	Thousands	% share
20 Natural Scientists	122	0.5
21 Engineers and Technologists	507	1.9
22 Health Professionals	233	0.9
23 Teaching Professionals	1211	4.7
24 Legal Professionals	75	0.3
25 Business and Financial Professionals	260	1.0
26 Architects, Town Planners and Surveyors	98	0.4
27 Librarians and Related Professionals	27	0.1
28 Miscellaneous Professionals (eg: clergy, psychologists and social workers)	126	0.5
TOTAL	2659	10.3

MAJOR GROUP 1: MANAGERS & ADMINISTRATORS

	Thousands	% share
12 Specialist Managers eg: marketing personnel	533	2.1
13 Financial Institute Managers and Civil Service Executive Officers	417	1.6

by the year 2000. By the end of the decade there will be over 10 million workers who can be classified as managers, professionals or associate professionals. Almost all of these will be involved in knowledge-intensive work and will require a high level of education and continuing professional development throughout their careers.

The traditional image of the professional is of someone working in a small business, as typified by the local solicitor with one office, the doctor working in a general practice with two or three partners or the country vet working single-handed. In fact, only a relatively small percentage of professionals work in the small business sector. Although the numbers of self-employed are growing – representing 10 per cent of the total number of professionals – the majority continue to work in larger organizations. For example, in the accountancy profession, of the 90,000 members of the Institute of Chartered Accountants almost 50,000 hold management positions mainly in the larger organizations (Swinson, 1991). Although there are several thousand small accountancy partnerships providing an invaluable service throughout the country, over half the professional employment in public practice is provided by the top five or six accountancy firms (Loveridge, 1991). The largest professional firms employ large numbers of people; for example KPMG Peat Marwick has more than 77,000 staff in 117 countries.

Overall more than 80 per cent of professionals in the UK work in larger firms. They are distributed throughout the economy, though the numbers vary from one industry sector to another. In food retailing, for example, a supermarket such as Sainsburys with a total workforce of 100,000, employs 316 professionals with a wide range of expertise in food hygiene and microbiology, distribution and logistics, information technology, personnel, estates management, finance, engineering, marketing and statistics. However, they form less than 1 per cent of the total workforce of the food retailing sector. In the software services sector, over 75 per cent are professional IT or business specialists, only 13 per cent are clerical staff and 11 per cent are in operational and strategic management.

There are large numbers of professionals in the public sector with, for example, over a million teachers and lecturers and approximately a quarter of a million health professionals.

PRESSURES AND TRENDS

The pressures for change which will affect all professionals to some degree over the next five years are discussed here under six headings: economic uncertainty; accountability; quality; maintenance of competence; towards flexible working; and information technology.

Economic uncertainty

As economic uncertainty intensifies, there will be an increasing emphasis on the role of professionals in wealth creation and on finding effective ways to manage the professional workforce for the benefit of the whole economy. Recent White Papers, such as 'Realising Our Potential: A Strategy for Science Engineering and Technology' (1993), all emphasize the importance of professionals for wealth creation in the evolving knowledge economy. Several recent studies have reinforced this view. For example, Bartel and Lichtenberg (1987) found that the productivity of highly educated workers relative to workers with low education is greater the more uncertainty there is in the production environment. As levels of uncertainty intensify, more resources must be devoted to gathering information on both the specialist needs of the customer and the technical possibilities. Bosworth and Wilson (1992) in a study for the ESRC, found that the profitability and growth of engineering firms is directly correlated to the employment of highly educated professional engineers and scientists. Mason and Wagner (1994) highlight the rapidly growing need for staff who can solve new and complex problems using analytical methods based on theoretical understanding rather than those who simply rely on past experience and trial and error. This growth in demand for high level skills and knowledge reflects intense competitive pressures. Manufacturers are obliged by their customers to achieve higher quality standards and meet ever more elaborate performance specifications as well as shortening product lead times and competing on price.

The challenge to management is to motivate the professional so that his or her contribution improves the performance and results of the whole organization. This entails formulating and communicating a clear vision for the future direction of the company, and empowerment of the workforce.

Career and personal development opportunities provided by companies for the professional must match their individual aspirations either in terms of performance related pay or self-development opportunities. To ensure the involvement and commitment of such a workforce, the organization has to shift the emphasis of its human resource policies towards facilitating the personal development of each individual, giving them more control over their individual destinies, development and working methods.

Accountability

The shift away from trusting professionals to do their work properly because they are professionally qualified, towards accountability, has resulted in the need for effective measures of competence, skill and service. This is welcomed by true professionals since it brings with it opportunities to establish more open relationships with customers and to enhance personal growth and development.

The traditional view of the professional is clearly conveyed by this quote from Drucker which emphasizes the autonomy of the professional:

> No one can motivate him (sic), he has to motivate himself. No one can direct him, he has to direct himself. Above all, no one can supervise him. He is guardian of his own standards, of his own performance and of his own objectives. He can be productive only if he is responsible for his own job. (Drucker, 1973)

Today the traditional role is under pressure from three main sources: the government, the consumer and the organization (see Figure 1.1).

New Expectations

Government ...
league tables, performance indicators

The Consumer ...
'Give me what I want, not what you think I want'.

The Organization ...
performance targets, appraisal

The Traditional View

No one can motivate him, he has to motivate himself. No one can direct him, he has to direct himself. Above all, no one can supervise him. He is guardian of his own standards, of his own performance and of his own objectives. He can be productive only if he is responsible for his own job.

Figure 1.1 *Pressures on the traditional view of the professional*

The Government

In the interests of free competition, the government seeks to create a level playing field through the removal of restrictive practices. Having succeeded with the trade unions, attention is now directed at the professional bodies. The government is also setting targets for a wide range of public sector professionals with performance indicators and league tables for universities, schools and hospitals. Although still in the early stages of development, the primitive quantitative-based methods in use today will soon be succeeded by more sophisticated and effective tools.

The Customer

Individual clients are now less willing to defer without question to expert opinion and expect to be fully informed with regard to the services on offer and the decisions taken by the professional on their behalf. They are much more likely to seek legal redress when the advice given turns out to be detrimental.

The Organization

Over 80 per cent of professionals work in large organizations. Those who manage them realize that to get the best from their professional workforce they must find ways of directing, controlling and coordinating their work without damaging the trust relationship, insulting their integrity and encroaching too much on their autonomy. Many attempts to manage professionals have failed because they tried to impose management techniques of control originating from outdated bureaucratic organizations. In most large organizations professionals, for the first time, are being given performance targets which dictate both the quality and quantity of their work. Such performance targets are backed up by appraisal interviews which determine how well a professional has performed.

Quality

One of the biggest shocks facing professionals is the way the quality of their work is being assessed and rewarded. In the public sector, government initiatives such as the Citizens Charter are imposing new levels of service delivery through demands for published standards for performance measurement, surveys of consumer opinion, and a better response rate to customer complaints. This has had a major effect so far on the working lives of thousands of doctors, teachers, and solicitors. These changes will soon affect social workers, policemen and other public sector professionals.

In the private sector, consumers are better informed, with more sophisticated demands and higher expectations of their professional advisers. This, together with government legislation to break monopolies, is forcing professionals such as solicitors to improve the quality of the service provided through the adoption of quality assurance systems such as BS 5750. In large organizations there are now service delivery contracts between professional departments such as IT and personnel and the business units they serve.

In the past, quality was regarded as part and parcel of professional advice and was beyond challenge. The old 'take it or leave it' and 'the professional knows best' attitudes are no longer appropriate; client needs and service delivery must be taken into account. All professionals now have to achieve measurable levels of service quality. Those who attempt to ignore the trend will find it imposed from outside. For example, the government imposes 'quality standards' on teachers; a car manufacturer decides to deal only with suppliers with BS 5750 accreditation; and the business manager in a large insurance company defines and insists on a quality service from the information technology department.

The 1990s will be a decade when quality and all that it implies for professionals will be a key issue. Achieving quality is difficult. Currently, most organizations appear to regard the introduction of quality improvement as an evolutionary process which involves three complementary stages:

- Client care programmes
- BS 5750
- Total Quality Management (TQM)

As attention is paid first to initiatives which involve the least disruption, we see a rush to establish client care programmes, followed by the implementation of BS 5750 standards, and finally a commitment to TQM. In large organizations, TQM may involve massive organizational upheaval and intense effort – some firms in the manufacturing sector have taken up to ten years to establish it. Other sectors, where the process is as yet unknown, will find that pressure to adopt quality standards is too great to permit a slow evolution and may face the prospect of a TQM revolution.

Maintenance of Competence

As the useful lifespan of knowledge gained in an initial degree or professional course declines, the need for continuing education becomes more urgent. Education and training must become a continuous lifelong process to keep abreast of change. All professionals need a blend of professional and managerial skills (see Figure 1.2). This blend of competences will vary from profession to profession and according to the individual's stage of development within the profession. Increasingly professionals are expected to have cross-functional skills to enable them to negotiate and communicate with other professionals. The kind of expertise required is gained through repeated involvement with a wide range of business situations and problems.

Professional Skills	Managerial Skills	Cross-functional Skills
Initial qualifications plus continuous updating in one's own professional area of expertise.	• Business • Inter-personal • Applied intellectual • Self-management and entrepreneurial	To enable professionals from different areas to reach a mutual understanding.

EXPERIENCE
Repeated involvement with a wide range of situations and problems.

Figure 1.2 *Changing skills required by professionals*

Professional Skills

Professionals are expected to have the expertise appropriate to their particular roles. In a rapidly changing environment, professional knowledge is becoming increasingly complex and specialized so individuals need constant updating to keep in touch with their area of specialization. In most professions, almost all the training budgets are spent on formal courses which are targeted at developing the knowledge-based skills of their particular disciplines. The professional bodies encourage this emphasis. As a consequence, provision for professional skill updating is widely available and well accepted. However, the other competences listed here are catered for in an unstructured, *ad hoc* way, through 'on-the-job training' and 'learning-by-doing'.

Managerial skills

Professionals need to develop a whole range of managerial skills which include:

- business skills to manage resources effectively and to understand the basic principles of marketing, information technology and finance;
- interpersonal skills to work effectively in groups and to liaise with a wide range of clients;
- applied intellectual skills to make appropriate decisions in a fast-changing environment;
- self-management and entrepreneurial skills to achieve results through individual initiative.

An awareness of the commercial features of the environment in which they operate, and the need to see themselves as business people as well as professionals, are increasingly emphasized today. This applies most obviously to self-employed professionals, whether working as sole practitioners, in partnerships, or as consultants. It also applies to those working in industry, who are under increasing pressure to be aware of the commercial pressures on the company they work for and the nature of the market in which they operate. They may be working within profit centres, and can no longer give detached, 'pure' advice without also having a view of the effect on the company's profitability. Professionals are therefore expected to have a wider range of skills than in the past.

> There is a vital core of management skills other than legal knowledge which needs to be taught. For example, some lawyers do not understand the basic disciplines of meeting, greeting and seating clients, nor of putting them at their ease and establishing the purpose of their meeting. (Helena Twist, in Fennel, 1989.)

Cross-functional Skills

Traditionally, professionals become more specialized as they progress, but increasingly they find that they are expected to have a grasp of broader issues too. Their work begins to overlap that of other professionals, with the result that they are asked to make decisions outside the immediate confines of their original specialism. For instance:

Ten years ago I was an expert in one field, I'm still an expert in that field but I'm also being asked to look at other things, and also I'm getting involved in law and litigation. I think as professionals we do overlap and the older we get the more experience we have and we do diversify. (Mechanical engineer)

Experience

Most professionals stress the value of experience. Experience enables professionals to recognize what knowledge is important, and how to access knowledge they do not possess if it turns out to be required. Therefore experience enables more effective use of existing and new knowledge.

I think the day you leave university another learning phase starts which is all to do with experience and gaining knowledge from actually doing things. The required competence is set by the market place and by your fellow professionals. If you don't have the required competence these days, you don't survive. (Civil engineer)

Towards Flexible Working

In their efforts to increase productivity, firms are restructuring their organizations to build in three kinds of flexibility:

- *career-life flexibility* in terms of the numbers employed, hours worked, rewards and degree of commitment to the firm;
- *functional flexibility* in terms of multi-skilling and cross-functional capability;
- *geographical flexibility* in terms of locating the means of production in areas of maximum return, that is, where the balance between costs and access to markets is optimal.

Research at Bristol University on career development for professionals (Watkins and Drury, 1994) examines the effect of each of the three kinds of flexibility on professional roles.

Career-life Flexibility

This trend, towards flexibility and performance-based criteria for recruitment and reward in the organization, is shaping a new kind of career pattern for the professional as well as the non-professional worker. The careers of the majority will increasingly be made up of a series of short-term assignments with a number of different firms, and recruitment will be highly selective. Charles

Handy (1989) uses the term 'portfolio career' in describing careers of this kind. The 'portfolio career' may include, for example, an early discovery period made up of short-term projects, culminating in a full-time, high-profile core position which may eventually lead to high-profile consultancy work; or it might be made up of a series of short-term assignments in different companies interspersed with periods of unemployment, self-employment and renewal through study.

Functional Flexibility

Enhancing customer focus is a key aim of restructuring for functional flexibility. If decision makers are not separated from the customer and from each other by functional barriers, their response to the customers' changing needs will be communicated and dealt with more quickly and effectively. Rigid job boundaries are disappearing and employees are expected to do more and to do a wider range of tasks – roles expand vertically within a single function or specialism or horizontally across a range of functions or specialities. As the boundaries shift, duties overlap, making coordinated team effort based on sharing of some resources essential. Core teams are involved in the ongoing, day-to-day work of the business; *ad hoc* or temporary teams are assembled to tackle special, project-based tasks.

Geographical Flexibility

Many firms in the developed Western world are relocating to areas where labour is cheaper and where regulations are less stringent. Initially, this involved the export of mainly menial work to the Far East and Latin America. However, workers in the West are now seeing the export of increasingly sophisticated work from all sectors. Work is flowing out to remote nations whose labour forces are now highly skilled. Factories and offices with 'state of the art' plant and office equipment are set up, some in virgin sites, and run by fewer people at a fraction of the costs incurred at old sites in the country of origin. To some extent this is counter-balanced by the continuing trend for American and Japanese companies to invest to increase their presence in the relatively affluent markets of high-wage countries in Europe and in Canada. However, with the collapse of the Communist regime in Eastern Europe as well as in China, some leading industrialists predict massive movements of increasingly highly skilled and professional work from the Western world (O'Reilly, 1992).

Information Technology

There are two major issues with regard to information technology which are of growing concern to professionals. First, information systems which are becoming increasingly more sophisticated can be used to monitor and control the work of professionals; second, as information technology takes over much of the routine clerical work, the knowledge intensity of the professional's work increases.

Information for Control or Development?

Technology provides information which can be used either to control the activities of the professional or to identify areas for improvement. For example, automation allows data to be gathered on the operations conducted by every surgeon in the country. Information can be generated which is used to compare success rates and cost-effectiveness, to identify areas of weakness or strength and cases for disciplinary action or opportunities for training in new surgical techniques. There is a tendency at the moment to use information as an instrument of control rather than development. Publicity surrounding many recent government initiatives often quotes unguarded comments, such as 'the incompetent will be weeded out', giving emphasis to the control aspect. However, these developments have the potential to be used in a positive way to identify areas for improvement.

Increased Knowledge Intensity

Many of the routine aspects of a professional's work can now be done more efficiently by computer, leading to important productivity gains in these areas and a concentration of professional expertise on high-level, more lucrative, work. The routine work can be devolved to support staff, an associate or paraprofessional with vocational and computer skills, thus increasing the range of work of which they are capable. IT which is harnessed to free the professional from the mundane so that he or she can make fuller use of higher-level skills and potential is an obvious opportunity to those able to take advantage of it. To others, it is a potential threat in terms of loss of income and loss of status. As the lower-level work is taken over by computers and associate professionals, the professional will have to spend an increasing amount of time working at a high level on more complex tasks. This has certain attractions in that this more demanding work is interesting and stimulating, but there are problems too in that working consistently at this level often results in high levels of stress and early burn out.

CONCLUSION

The number of professionals has grown rapidly, particularly in the late 1970s and 80s, so that they now constitute approximately 15 per cent of the population. As other groups such as nurses aspire to professional status, and as the expansion of new and old professions continues, it is predicted that by the year 2000 almost 30 per cent of the population will be classified as professional. It is the fastest growing occupational group. Currently most professionals work in large organizations and they are heavily represented in the public sector in such areas as health, education and local government.

Pressures for accountability from government, consumers and organizations will lead to more stringent and effective measures of both the quality and quantity of the professional's work. Education, training and career development must become a continuous lifelong process if the professional is to keep abreast of change. The development of cross-functional and interpersonal skills will enable them to work effectively in groups and to negotiate and communicate with a wide range of professionals from other disciplines. All will need managerial and entrepreneurial skills to survive in an increasingly commercial environment. As competition from the Pacific Rim intensifies, they will need to plan flexible career paths which keep new or alternative opportunities always in view. While advances in information technology pose some threats, they will free the professional from routine to concentrate on high-level, interesting and demanding work.

In these times of economic uncertainty, the professional's wealth-creating potential will be determined by how well he or she can adapt to meet the pressures described.

REFERENCES

Bartel, A and Lichtenberg, F (1987) 'The comparative advantage of educated workers in implementing new technology', *The Review of Economic Statistics*.

Bosworth, D and Wilson, R (1992) *Qualified Scientists and Engineers and Economic Performance*, Institute of Employment Research, University of Warwick, Coventry.

Cabinet Office (1993) White Paper, *Realising Our Potential: A strategy for science engineering and technology*, London, HMSO.

Drucker, P (1973) *Management*, Harper & Row, New York.

Fennel, E (1989) 'Lessons for the learned', *The Times*, 7 March.

Handy, C (1989) *The Age of Unreason*, Hutchinson, London.

Loveridge, R (1991) 'Judgement, standards and Ethics – Lawyers and accountants as carriers of order' in Lee, GL (ed.) *The Changing Professions: accountancy and law*, Aston Business School, Research Institute.

Mason, G and Wagner, K (1994) 'High-level skills and industrial competitiveness: Postgraduate engineers and scientists in Britain and Germany', Report No. 6, NIESR London.

O'Reilly, B (1992) 'Today's Global Workforce', *Fortune*.

Swinson, C (1991) 'The professions and 1992', in Lee, GL (ed.), *The Changing Professions: accountancy and law*, Aston Business School, Research Institute.

Watkins, JW and Drury, L (1994) *Positioning for the Unknown: career development for professionals in the 1990s*, University of Bristol.

Watkins, JW, Drury, L and Preddy, D (1992) *From Evolution to Revolution: The pressures on professional life in the 1990s*, University of Bristol.

Wilson, RA (1991) *Review of the Economy and Employment (Occupational Assessment)*, University of Warwick, Institute for Employment Research.

2

CPD in the Construction Industry

Dennis Neale

INTRODUCTION

Bearing in mind the disciplinary separation and adversarial attitudes of the various professions in the construction industry it is perhaps surprising that an outstanding feature of continuing professional development (CPD) in construction has been the extent of commonality of action among the professional institutions. This is largely due to the formation in 1975 of the York Centre for the Development of Continuing Education for the Building Professions and its successor, the CPD in Construction Group, formed in 1980.

THE CPD IN CONSTRUCTION GROUP

During its 14 years of existence the Group has:

- developed the term 'continuing professional development' (CPD) and its definition, now adopted by many organizations both inside and outside construction
- acted as an information exchange on CPD
- given advice and encouragement for the development of CPD by professional institutions, firms and individuals
- acted as a pressure group on government and other agencies for support for CPD
- established links with CPD providers in both the public and private sectors
- published a quarterly 'CPD Newsletter'
- produced a series of multi-disciplinary audio-visual CPD packages under the general theme 'Better Building'

41

- produced a CPD kit, audio tapes and other publications
- carried out a survey of tax reliefs for CPD in a number of over-seas countries and pressured government to give tax relief for CPD that is paid for by the individual
- carried out a survey of monitoring activities and given advice to members on this aspect of CPD.

The Group amalgamated with the Construction Industry Council with effect from 1 January 1994 and is now a Standing Committee of the Council while still retaining its own identity as a Group. These are now 20 professional institutions with a total membership of 325,000 and seven organizations representing some 1,000 firms in membership of the Group, a powerful and influential body for the further development of CPD.

CPD AND THE PROFESSIONAL INSTITUTIONS

In the past, professional institutions have traditionally offered members a range of activities – lectures, seminars, workshops, information papers, journals etc – which today are regarded as part of the provision for CPD. The take-up was limited and there was no formal system of CPD.

Professional institutions have long had an implicit responsibility to secure and maintain the standards of competence of their members. During the past 10–15 years the professional institutions in construction have been developing a formal *obligatory* CPD scheme with two objectives: to motivate their members to identify the need for and to undertake systematic programmes of CPD, and to assist members to carry out their CPD.

The assistance to members takes a variety of forms, eg:

Issue of guidelines, record books, etc.
Provision of courses, lecture meetings, seminars, etc.
Issue of certificates of attendance
Provision of courses linked to Certificates of Competence
Technical information services, eg, articles in journals
Production of distance/open learning material
Formation of CPD study centres
Accreditation of short courses/course providers
Data banks, directories of CPD facilities, bibliographies
Advice, counselling.

Table 2.1 shows the status of CPD in the professional institutions in the construction industry:

Table 2.1 *The status of CPD in the construction industry*

Professional institution	CPD Status	Minimum CPD per year
Architects and Surveyors Institute 5,500 members	Obligatory	20 hrs
Association of Building Engineers 4,200 members	Obligatory	20 hrs
British Institute of Architectural Technologists 6,200 members	Obligatory	35 hrs
Chartered Institute of Building 33,000 members	Obligatory	35 hrs
Chartered Institution of Building Services Engineers 15,250 members	Obligatory	30 hrs
Institute of Building Control 3,700 members	Obligatory	15 hrs
Institute of Clerks of Works 3,700 members	Recommended	20 hrs
Institute of Highway Incorporated Engineers 2,500 members	Recommended	35 hrs
Institute of Maintenance and Building Management 2,400 members	Obligatory	20 hrs
Institute of Plumbing 14,000 members	Voluntary	Not currently specified
Institution of Civil Engineers 79,660 members	Obligatory	5 days (35 hrs)
Institute of Civil Engineering Surveyors 3,050 members	Obligatory	25 points varying with activity
Institution of Structural Engineers 21,526 members	Obligatory	20 hrs
Landscape Institute 3,634 members	Obligatory	20 hrs
Royal Institute of British Architects 28,000 members	Obligatory	35 hrs
Royal Institution of Chartered Surveyors 90,576 members	Obligatory	20 hrs
Society of Surveying Technicians 5,000 members	Obligatory	20 hrs
Royal Town Planning Institute 18,000 members	Obligatory	25 hrs

The meaning of *Obligatory* is that: members of professional institutions are required to observe the Royal Charter/byelaws/rules/regulations of their institution. Applicants for admission to membership are normally required to complete and sign an application form which includes an undertaking on the lines – 'I hereby undertake to observe the byelaws/rules/regulations of the institution for the time being in force'. If the institute has a byelaw/rule/regulation requiring CPD, or subsequently adopts one, the member is obligated by the undertaking, previously given, to observe its provisions; thus – CPD is 'obligatory'.

SOME OF THE LESSONS THAT HAVE BEEN LEARNED

From the extensive experience of CPD in the industry a number of significant points have been identified.

Preparation of Personal Development Plan

CPD needs are unique to each individual and it is for each individual and his/her firm to decide what CPD should be undertaken, how and when. The first step is to make a realistic and critical appreciation of strengths and deficiencies in performance, for the present job and for foreseeable future roles.

A *Personal Development Plan* should then be prepared. This should include objectives, priorities and time-scale taking account of the firm's objectives, requirements of the professional institution, personal interests and career intentions. Thereafter, it is essential to review the Personal Development Plan at regular intervals and to record action that is taken to secure its objectives.

Most of the professional institutions in construction provide career planners/diaries to assist members to draw up their personal development plans and to record the CPD undertaken. The CPD in Construction Group provides a CPD Planner and Record for those who for one reason or another do not propose/are not able to use a particular institution's publication.

Means of undertaking CPD

It is sometimes thought that the only way of carrying out CPD is by attendance at seminars, short courses, workshops, etc., requiring absence from work. This is not so; there are many ways in which knowledge and skill can be improved and personal qualities developed. The decision about the most suitable way and the amount and coverage of the CPD to be undertaken, must rest with the individual and his/her firm. There is now a general acceptance that CPD may be carried out by any of the following means:

Technical and professional conferences, lectures, seminars, workshops, study tours and short courses

Courses for higher degrees

Firms' in-house discussions, research activities and inter-firm studies

Open/distance learning (video packages, audio tapes, slide/tape packages, correspondence courses, etc.)

Private study including systematic study of the literature (not casual reading)

Preparing articles for publication

Teaching (for those not in teaching posts)

Practice (for those in teaching posts)

Preparing papers and contributing to technical meetings and study groups

Examining, tutoring

Job rotation, secondment.

The CPD in Construction Group's definition of CPD which follows has two parts – the first concerned with the improvement of knowledge and skill in a professional context and the second concerned with development of personal qualities:

The systematic maintenance, improvement and broadening of knowledge and skill and the development of personal qualities necessary for the execution of professional and technical duties throughout the practitioner's working life.

The development of personal qualities, such as skill in human relations, may be achieved by activities outside one's professional life, for example through involvement in service for a voluntary organization.

Monitoring

Surveys have shown that two rather different systems of monitoring are being employed by the professional institutions in construction; these are:

1) *Questionnaire*
   Designed to identify the number of hours of CPD being undertaken; the means by which it was undertaken; the preferred mode; difficulties experienced; choice of topics;
2) *Scrutiny of CPD Records*
   Calling in of a number of Personal Development Plans/Logbooks from a sample of members selected at random.

Some of the advantages and disadvantages of the two systems are as follows:

Questionnaire	Scrutiny of CPD records
More of an 'information' scheme	More of a 'policing' scheme
Less opportunity to detect and pursue 'unsatisfactory' cases	Opportunity to pursue 'unsatisfactory' cases
Lends itself to a large number of respondents	Tends to be prohibitive of large numbers
Processing requires relatively little resource	Labour-intensive if scrutiny is exacting
Information produced about difficulties experienced	No information about difficulties experienced
No means of knowing how CPD plans and records are actually being maintained by individuals	Insight into production of PDPs and maintenance of records by certain individuals
Little if any proof of the CPD being carried out	Reasonable proof of CPD being (or not being) carried out
Facility for suggestions of topics of interest, etc.	No information about topics of interest.

Experience has shown that members are keen to see a tough stance being taken on monitoring investigations until it affects them, when it is then seen as a bureaucratic 'big brother' activity. The tone and style of the approach is thus all important.

Generally, individuals demonstrate misconceptions rather than outright obstructionism. Members need to be reminded of the CPD 'message' and the message needs to be updated and promoted regularly by a variety of means. As CPD becomes more readily accepted, the validity of the quantative measurement becomes more questionable and greater consideration needs to be given to the qualitative aspects.

Validation of CPD provision/providers

A demand by members for the validation of short courses and distance learning material is an inevitable development following the introduction of formal CPD schemes. So far as short courses are concerned, this is an ephemeral area – there are many hundreds; some provided at short notice with little publicity, some offered but not run. Even the provision of a database of current material presents overwhelming problems and effective assessment of quality and relevance becomes an impossibility.

What is important, however, is that the course provider should give, in the publicity about the event or distance learning material, sufficient information for the individual firm to make a reasonable judgement about whether the event or item is relevant to their CPD needs. The CPD in Construction Group has issued 'Guidance Notes for CPD Providers' which outlines the information that should be included – a clear idea of the aim, content and quality of the event/item.

A number of institutions provide lists of short courses and distance learning in periodic catalogues. A disclaimer about the quality and relevance of the items is usually included. As an alternative to lists of courses, certain institutions provide lists of course *providers* which have been assessed for quality.

Acceptable topics

The preparation of a list of approved topics was originally considered by certain institutions to be an essential part of the CPD scheme. This denies, however, the duty of the individual or firm to carry out an objective assessment of need and to draw up a programme of topics designed to satisfy that need. Moreover the topics included in an institution's list may be inappropriate for the CPD needs of a particular member. For example, a list of topics about architecture may be inappropriate for an architect who wishes to develop knowledge and skill in management.

It is now generally accepted that lists of 'compulsory' subjects may defeat the whole purpose of CPD. On the other hand lists which are offered in an endeavour to assist a member are part of the help that an institution may give.

CONCLUSION

Professional people can no longer depend on their initial education and training to equip them for their entire working life. Sustained professional competence requires continuing professional development of the individual and of the organization. Increasingly, there is a recognition that updating of existing knowledge and skill and the development of new knowledge and skill are a part of professional life. The development of personal qualities is also essential as part of career development. Individual practitioners, their employers, the professional bodies, and teaching institutions are increasingly aware that CPD is a joint responsibility requiring shared commitment and action.

The increasing complexity of construction; the need for improved performance, radical changes in materials, techniques and systems; changes in the traditional roles of the 'building team'; consumer protection; quality control; developments in information technology; the challenge – and the opportunities – of the 1990s are all contributing to the need for what is being called 'lifelong learning'. CPD is the means to the end – the end being improved performance. CPD is not new. What is new is its greater importance and urgency and the need to have a determined and systematic approach to it.

The current output of the construction industry is some £48 billion per annum, representing one-eighth of the UK Gross Domestic Product. The total labour force is 1.5 million. The industry is thus an important one both sociologically and economically. In an increasingly competitive world it is vital that the industry, its firms and individuals maintain and improve their performance and thus their economic competitiveness. This is the purpose of continuing professional development. To undertake it makes good business sense. Increasingly it is seen to be a natural and essential part of career development by the younger professional; the older professional needs to recognize the need for it as formal technical education becomes a distant memory.

3

Professional Bodies and Continuing Professional Development

Clare Rapkins

INTRODUCTION

Based upon research carried out in 1992 and published in *Professional Standards and Competence: A Survey of Continuing Education for the Professionals* (Madden and Mitchell, 1993), this chapter will highlight and analyse the role of professional bodies in Continuing Professional Development (CPD) including: the instigation of CPD policy; the nature of the CPD policy put into place; the form of provision accepted; the nature and target of the promotion of the CPD policy; the monitoring and evaluation of subsequent compliance; and take-up by members.

Two models of CPD policy and practice will be examined and three examples of current good practice by professional bodies will be outlined. The chapter will describe the importance of associated areas of research in terms of developing models of best CPD policy and practice. This will include research into adult learning, and research into the changing pressures on professionals in the 1990s. The chapter will close with recommendations to professional bodies for building and administering effective schemes for continuing professional development.

THE PROFESSIONS AND CONTINUING PROFESSIONAL DEVELOPMENT

The professions are subject to the same pressures as other occupations when considering responses to: changes in technology and knowledge; demands for quality and accountability; and recruitment from a diminishing pool of school and college leavers. These factors, together with the need for an overall improvement in economic competitiveness in response to deregulation and the EU marketplace, have impressed upon employers and the government the need for policy and structuring of continuing education in the workplace. Professional bodies have joined the push for continuing education among qualified, practising professionals through CPD which has been defined by the CPD in Construction Group as:

> The systematic maintenance, improvement and broadening of knowledge and skill and the development of personal qualities necessary for the execution of professional and technical duties throughout the practitioner's working life.

This definition highlights three crucial elements of CPD for the practitioner: that it is systematic or planned; that it is about broadening and deepening knowledge, skill and expertise, in addition to updating it; and, that it is a *lifelong* commitment to continuing professional competence.

Professional development has, until recently, been a response to the need to meet specific and immediate needs for the updating of technological knowledge. The changing demands now being placed upon the professional (as outlined earlier) have led to a recognition of the need for a planned and structured approach to learning for work. It is only since the early 1980s that professional bodies have assumed a proactive role in CPD.

The following is an outline of survey research carried out by the author and designed to examine the role of professional bodies in CPD policy and practice. The results and their interpretation are used to describe current good practice of CPD amongst UK professional bodies, and to make recommendations for best practice in the future.

SURVEY OF CURRENT CONTINUING PROFESSIONAL DEVELOPMENT

The aim of the research was to review current CPD for a range of professions in the United Kingdom and to identify characteristics for effective CPD provision in the light of current policies and future requirements for CPD and by comparison with theories of adult learning and research into the change in the professions in the 1990s.

Research Methodology

A sample of 20 was used for the purposes of the study, comprising 17 professional bodies and three national councils (all of which have responsibility for education and training across the spectrum of their professions). The sample represented a cross-section of contemporary professions in respect of occupational field, age and perceived professional status.

Each of the 20 bodies was designated either 'old and established'; or 'new and/or developing' and categorized by occupational area. The six occupational fields were: construction; engineering; finance and law; management; medicine; and social and personal health science. Information about CPD policy and practice was extracted by the author, using a standard survey framework questionnaire, from documentation supplied by the professional body. Further information was collected from 16 professional bodies by means of in-depth interviews.

The survey framework and the interviews concentrated on five areas of investigation: the profession and professional body; the organization of CPD; the structure of CPD provision; the promotion of CPD; the monitoring and evaluation of CPD.

Models of CPD Provision

The results of the survey suggested differences in CPD policy and provision between the 'old and established' professional bodies, and those that were 'new and/or developing'. The contrasting reasons for instigating a CPD policy and the subsequent definition and function of CPD appeared to exert direct influence over the nature of the policy for CPD that was adopted by the professional body.

Models of CPD provision were developed on the basis of these differences. Two models are described: the 'sanctions model' typical of the 'old and established' professional bodies; and, the 'benefits model' characterized by the 'new and/or developing' professions. These models provide the foundation to identifying characteristics of effective CPD provision.

The 'sanctions model' of CPD is adopted by professional bodies (some regulatory) that have mandatory CPD policies and rely on the threat of sanctions when the requirements of this policy are not complied with. Such bodies instigate a CPD policy in order to demonstrate standards of professional competence and define CPD items as the updating of technical skill and knowledge. The success of the policy is measured in terms of compliance by members with the specific requirements of the policy rather than any change in a practitioner's knowledge, skill and expertise that is the prime outcome of the learning process (see the Institute of Actuaries and the Royal Institution of Chartered Surveyors examples that follow).

Other professional bodies which have, in general, introduced CPD more recently and are less well-established professional groupings, have adopted voluntary CPD policies. These professional bodies have instigated CPD in an attempt to gain, or improve, professional standing and status and to compete more effectively with older and better established professions within their occupational field. They adopt a CPD policy that provides benefits and/or *rewards* for those who take part in it, sometimes in terms of academic or competence-based qualifications, eg, English National Board for Nursing, Midwifery and Health Visitors' Advanced Award (Madden and Mitchell, 1993, pp. 37–9). We have termed this the 'benefits model' of CPD (see the Institute of Personnel Management example that follows). Such professional bodies place emphasis on the *implementing of learning in practice* and on all the partners in the CPD process (individual practitioner, employer, provider and professional body) assuming defined and specific responsibilities. In addition, these professional bodies emphasize the importance of the outcome of CPD for practice, though the professional body itself is still slow to define the means by which individuals may evaluate the outcomes of their learning for practice.

The major disadvantage of a voluntary CPD policy is that those with most to gain from CPD are least likely to do it. While mandatory policies lack flexibility and individuality they are a means of ensuring that *all* qualified members have the opportunity to be exposed to new techniques and professional competences.

EXAMPLES OF GOOD CPD PRACTICE

The Royal Institution of Chartered Surveyors (RICS)

The RICS is an 'old and established' professional body with 63,000 members, which has adopted the sanctions model of CPD.

Good practice is characterized by:

- the employment of a CPD Coordinator since 1989, and membership of the CPD in Construction Group (stressing inter-professionalism)
- well-defined aims and a definition of CPD: to produce well-rounded, motivated practitioners with continuing competence to practice; and 'to update and develop knowledge and skills in business, managerial and personal, as well as technical, areas'
- an obligatory CPD policy since 1991
- CPD requirements in RICS Byelaw Regulations
- remedial and ongoing advice and guidance on compliance to ensure non-compliance does not become an issue
- recommendation of 20 hours of CPD per annum, but a 60-hour requirement over 3 years allows flexibility
- recognition of a range of CPD activities
- being a major provider of a wide range of CPD activities itself including the use of audio cassette updates
- stipulating that only two-thirds of annual CPD can be private study and then only when this is planned
- recommending that practitioners involve employers in the planning of CPD.

The Institute of Actuaries

This is a small but distinct regulatory and 'old and well established' professional body with 2,650 members, adopting a primarily sanctions model approach to CPD. Good practice is characterized by:

- the appointment of a Director of Education who provides for a continuum of education with responsibility for initial and post-qualification education
- well-defined aims for the CPD policy: the need to safeguard its professional standards, reduce indemnity insurance and rise to the challenge of increased competitiveness
- CPD policy being mandatory where it can be: newly qualified actuaries; those wishing to upgrade membership; those holding a practising certificate
- strong networks (as a small profession) allowing ideas to permeate quickly and successfully
- dividing CPD into two categories – formal and informal – the former covering technical areas and the latter development in non-practice fields

- monitoring by sample – 20 per cent per annum of the records kept by those who have mandatory CPD requirements
- not evaluating courses as this suggests endorsement which it believes is best left to the individual.

Institute of Personnel Management (IPM)

The IPM is a non-regulatory and 'new and developing' professional body which adopts the benefits model of CPD. Good practice is characterized by:

- an initial policy statement in 1984 for all those in work, plus a current agreed policy
- the emphasis on individual responsibility for, and management of, learning and the integration of learning into work and practice
- consideration of the needs of the employer
- recognition of the importance of individual learning needs, learning styles and learning opportunities
- an emphasis on competence in practice rather than accumulation of knowledge
- a voluntary policy but evidence of CPD as essential for upgrading membership
- pre-empting problems of take-up by promoting the benefits of CPD to the individual practitioner and the employer and acceptance of a wide range of activities to count as CPD
- emphasis on the outcomes of CPD recorded through a personal portfolio, rather than the number of hours of CPD undertaken.

COMPARATIVE THEORETICAL AND APPLIED RESEARCH

The research described below has practical implications for CPD in terms of recommendations to professional bodies about the best learning process and learning content of CPD.

Cognitive Theories of Adult Learning

CPD aims to enhance professional competence so that professionals practise most effectively throughout their career.

By applying theoretical and practical analyses of adult learning literature we are able to deduce that if CPD is to be effective it must: meet the learning needs of professionals and their employers; be flexible enough to allow individual learning styles to be accommodated; and provide a number of learning opportunities (Madden and Mitchell, 1993, pp. 49–54).

Learning Needs

Practitioners will have different needs according to where they are employed, their role, and the stage of their career. In order to meet these needs the content of CPD must cover:

- updating and broadening of technical knowledge and skill
- developing skills used by the professional, eg, communication, interpersonal, information technology and negotiation skills
- preparation for changing professional roles, eg, developing managerial, financial and management skills
- development of professional specialist expertise.

Employers must also be taken into account. The role of the employer as an instigator, a facilitator and a funder of CPD cannot be overestimated and CPD must certainly reflect commercial and competitive realities.

CPD must be a partnership to include the players who stand to benefit from it: as well as the professional and employer, there is also the professional body, which instigates the policy and places requirements on its professionals; and society with its interest in high quality professional expertise.

All learning for CPD should be judged on the basis of its fitness for purpose. This is evaluated in terms of its effectiveness in updating and developing skills for practice. A training needs analysis and assessment of the effectiveness in enhancing practitioner's performance is appropriate for any model of CPD.

Learning Style

Professionals are adult learners and as such they are voluntary learners (Knowles, in Madden and Mitchell, 1993). Not only does this mean that they learn best when the content of learning is relevant and has direct application to practice, but also that the process of learning must fit self-directed and self-motivated autonomous individuals. Adults learn by building upon existing experience and so the process of education or training should be practice- and problem-orientated and facilitatory rather than didactic (Madden and Mitchell, 1993, p. 54).

Learning Opportunities

CPD must be appropriate in its content and process and in the range of forms offered: accessibility, day/evening, venue and cost must all be considered by the practitioner and employer when making decisions about CPD. Learning opportunities can also be offered by work-based activities that do not need time away or large course fees.

The Changing Professional Environment

CPD must take into account, and indeed drive and be driven by, the significant changes facing the professions in the next decade. Research suggests (Watkins *et al.*, 1992) that technological, social, economic, political and cultural developments are likely to affect work practice for professionals.

Increases in the use and integration of information technology into work remove some of the more humdrum and time-consuming work of professionals; the delayering and down-sizing of large organizations means less opportunity for 'upward' career progression, and the likelihood that work will be project-based and multi-disciplinary.

In addition, accountability to the consumers of professional services and the drive for quality together with the removal of restrictive practices increase the need to keep up to date. All these factors imply the need for different types of knowledge and skill for tomorrow's professional with, for example, core communication, interpersonal negotiation, team working and selling skills coming to the fore. CPD policy must not only reflect such changes, but should be proactive in preparing professionals at all levels to practise effectively in this new environment and retain competitive edge.

CHARACTERISTICS OF BEST CPD POLICY AND PRACTICE

By examining current CPD policy and practice in the context of theories into adult learning and the changing pressures facing professionals in their working lives, we are able to describe three groups of characteristics that influence best CPD policy and practice:

- Policy and conditions for CPD
- CPD provision
- Monitoring, quality assurance and evaluation of CPD.

Policy and Conditions for CPD Policy

A professional body must have a CPD policy that clearly defines the aims of CPD and how these aims can be achieved. The policy itself may vary according to the nature and needs of the profession but it is best when it provides for structured, systematic CPD throughout a professional career.

Analysis of Professional Competence
To produce a CPD policy a body must have some awareness of the knowledge and skill required by members in their jobs. An analysis of professional competence would allow professional bodies to make informed recommendations to professionals about what knowledge, skill or expertise needs to be developed or maintained at particular times in their career.

Good CPD Culture
In establishing an environment favourable to CPD there should be acknowledgement of, and the building of, partnerships between all those who will benefit from and have responsibility for CPD: the individual professional, the professional body, the employer, providers and society.

As the instigator of CPD policy, the professional body plays a crucial role. Professional bodies should act as ambassadors for continuous learning and encourage practitioners to start to think about CPD during initial professional education and to establish a synthesis of initial and continuing education.

CPD Provision

CPD Content
Attention needs to be given to updating but also extending and deepening knowledge, skills and expertise. Technical knowledge must be covered but also personal and management skills.

Developing Provider Partnerships
The professional body should collaborate both with a range of providers and other professional bodies to offer the widest range and depth of CPD provision.

Forms of CPD
Where, when and how CPD is provided must suit the individual practitioner. Emphasis should be on flexibility to include on-the-

job learning, short courses and modular or open learning. CPD should meet the practitioners' and employers' needs in terms of different learning needs, styles and opportunities.

Promoting and Marketing CPD
Although it is important to persuade practitioners to invest in their own CPD it is also crucial that employers are informed of the value and benefit of CPD to the organization in order that the best partnerships between employers, practitioners and the professional body can be forged.

Cost
CPD should enhance competence in practice and therefore cost can vary considerably. Some of the most effective CPD takes place on the job, with little or no direct cost to the employer for fees or lost professional time.

Monitoring, Quality Assurance and Evaluation

Monitoring of Practitioners' CPD
Resources should be concentrated on promoting the benefits and process of CPD and developing new CPD services, so where mandatory CPD policies exist, a quota monitoring system is advised, keeping monitoring cost to a minimum.

Quality Assurance and Evaluation of CPD Provision
Most professional bodies already devolve responsibility for evaluation of CPD providers and provision to the professional. This is sensible given that CPD needs to fit the individual needs of the practitioner.

RECOMMENDATIONS FOR PROFESSIONAL BODIES

To achieve effective CPD, ie best CPD practice, action is required at both the strategic and the operational level. It also requires different actions by the different CPD partners: the practitioners, the professional body, the employers, the providers and government.

Finally, we make recommendations about the characteristics of effective CPD, which professional bodies should take control of:

■ the development of CPD policy – in partnership with employers and government

- analysis of professional competence – by consultation with the National Council for Vocational Qualifications
- good CPD culture – in partnership with employers and government
- developing provider partnerships
- a range of CPD options – through liaison with external providers
- promotion and marketing of the CPD policy to all partners
- monitoring practitioners' CPD.

REFERENCES

Madden, CA and Mitchell, VA (1993) *Professional Standards and Competence: A survey of continuing education for the professionals*, Department for Continuing Education, University of Bristol.

Watkins, J, Drury, L and Preddy, D (1992) *From Evolution to Revolution: The pressures on professional life in the 1990s*, Department for Continuing Education, University of Bristol.

4

The Rabbits and the Lettuces – The Dual Role of Professional Bodies

Nigel Hughes

> People tend not to be convinced that the rabbits should be given the job of guarding the lettuces.
>
> Ian Hay Davidson

Those professions to which the public turns for advice, such as accountants and lawyers, are finding that a change is coming about in their relationship with their clients. Once treated with awe, even reverence, their advice was taken as if it were handed down on tablets of stone even if, perhaps especially if, the client was unable to understand it. They now find their advice questioned. Second opinions may be sought. And if something goes wrong, writs may start to fly.

One of the reasons for this is that there have been some spectacular failures of late. Those with the highest profile have been the corporate collapses – Maxwell, Polly Peck, British & Commonwealth among others – and the fallout from these has kept firms and their professional indemnity insurers rather busy. As a chartered accountant myself I tend to notice the kind of events where my profession gets a mention, but other professions have also had their share of bad press.

One effect of these events has been growing concern over the fact that the professional bodies serve a dual role – that of trade association for their membership and also regulator and watchdog of professional standards. In spite of having a membership made up exclusively of rabbits, the professional body also asks to be trusted with the task of guarding the lettuces.

Once the professional body has decided that it will be accountable for regulating the standard of competence among its members, it has to be seen to be doing something about it. Over the past decade complex and expensive mechanisms of regulation and enforcement have evolved. These usually have to be backed up by a system of authorization and monitoring with penalties for those found not to be up to the mark. The first step on this road taken by my own professional body, the Institute of Chartered Accountants in England and Wales (ICAEW), was the establishment of a policy on Continuing Professional Education – the equivalent of CPD – in 1978. At the time this was generally accepted as being quite a radical step forward in the maintenance of professional competence and all that was required. But CPD arrangements are now usually incorporated as simply a part of a more complex and expensive regulatory system.

There is a nagging doubt that true professionals should not really need any encouragement to keep up to date. If they fail to do this, they cannot be true professionals. This doubt leads me to three key questions about the professional bodies and their CPD rules:

- Is a CPD policy really necessary?
- Is the kind of CPD system usually operated effective?
- If a policy is necessary, but systems are usually ineffective, what should be put in their place?

To answer the first question first and quite simply, I believe that CPD policies are necessary because these matters are as much about public confidence as anything else. Therefore, it is important for professional bodies to be *seen* to be doing something. A CPD policy is one comparatively simple and cheap way of demonstrating a commitment to professional competence. The difficulty then arises as to how you operate a CPD policy once you have one. Before suggesting what is wrong with current systems and looking at alternatives, it would seem to be sensible to take a more detailed look at what is currently done by the professional bodies.

The way it usually works is this: the professional body sets a target quota of CPD for those of its members who wish to continue to serve the public and hold practising certificates. This is usually construed by the membership as being enforced attendance at courses, because the quota is usually set in terms of a required number of hours over a period, and the easiest way to fulfil the required number of hours is to attend a course.

I would like to question the effectiveness of this type of CPD regime in actually delivering the intended result. This result may be defined as 'increasing the degree of certainty that the public will receive the service it expects from members'.

WHAT A CPD SYSTEM SHOULD DO

What then is it the public expects? I suggest that the deceptively simple answer is that the client expects competent advice in return for a reasonable fee. Market forces ought to look after the 'reasonable fee', but a CPD system ought to play a part in the competence aspect.

It is at this point that the professional body comes up against the two major problems of making the CPD requirement effective.

- How do you ensure your members fulfil their CPD commitment? – the compliance problem, and
- how can you be sure that it does them, and hopefully the public they serve, any good? – the relevance problem.

After all, if you just say they should go on courses, what is to stop them attending flower arranging or scuba diving courses?

The twin problems of CPD

Compliance
Professional bodies find it comparatively easy to address the compliance problem and we will look in more detail at the approach the ICAEW has taken over the past 16 years or so and draw some conclusions from this.

Relevance
The much more difficult problem is the question of relevance. To maintain competence the professional's CPD must be gained in areas which are pertinent to the needs of the clients. This too we will examine in some detail.

I believe that the quota and points systems currently used are not effective and may even be counter-productive, in that they tend to steer the professional towards training which he or she may well not really need and, in consequence, away from training which is relevant. We will then make some suggestions about how a better result could be achieved.

Let us start by looking in some detail at how one professional body – ICAEW – has tackled the CPD problem over the last 16 years.

THE ICAEW EXPERIENCE

Background

In 1978 the ICAEW began to operate a CPD policy, which has been gradually revised over the years. The introduction of compulsory CPD was a radical change in policy and, as is normal in such cases, it was perceived that to make the new policy retrospective would be unfair on those who had passed through the old system. Some anomalies were therefore tolerated which are only now being addressed.

In order to enforce a compulsory CPD policy some 'triggers' or 'teeth' have to be found – sanctions which will be respected by the membership. In the ICAEW's case such sanctions were to be the granting or withholding of Practising Certificates, which signify the right of a member to engage in public practice, and Fellowships, which signify a certain degree of experience. These would only be granted to those who satisfied the CPD requirements. ICAEW has tried a number of different approaches to controlling CPD, as outlined below.

Accreditation and full reporting of CPD

The first approach was to insist that in order to fulfil their CPD quota, members should only attend courses which had been accredited by the Institute as providing valid CPD. Members would also have to make an annual return to the Institute of the courses they had attended.

This approach was far from successful. The validation process resulted in large numbers of course providers submitting vast quantities of course specifications to the Institute for approval. The Institute simply did not have the resources to do anything meaningful in the validation process and in any event it was impossible to provide people with the necessary technical competence to do the validating. So it became a rubber-stamping exercise, was recognized as serving no purpose and was abandoned.

This validation process has various other disadvantages, the principal one being that someone attending a validated course gets the CPD points whereas someone attending an equally good, or maybe better, non-validated course, does not. This is self-evidently unfair and instantly raises suspicions in the minds of the membership about price differentials between validated and non-validated courses.

The full reporting of CPD each year also caused a problem. If it was to be a genuine exercise to ensure that members were complying with the rules, each return would need to be checked. The paperwork would have to be filed and stored. Administrative procedures would need to be introduced to chase up those who failed to make the return. Not surprisingly, this idea was also soon dropped.

Annual confirmation of compliance

The next approach was to require the membership to maintain records of CPD and to confirm annually on a tear-off slip provided for the purpose, that they had done their duty.

By this time the CPD requirement had been modified. The quota of hours of course attendance had been converted to a points system which is rather more flexible and this is still the system in force. It requires members to achieve 150 CPD points each year. One point is scored per hour of unstructured CPD – technical reading and research; three points are scored per hour of structured CPD – course attendance, following structured distance learning packages, etc. This system at least has the capacity for giving members credit for technical reading and genuine attempts to do the necessary research for the day-to-day servicing of their clients' needs. It is still a long way short of genuinely attacking the relevance problem, as we shall see.

The Current System

Eventually the annual confirmation idea was dropped. Members now have to fulfil their CPD commitment following the points system outlined above, and maintain records of the CPD they do. Although these are open to inspection either on demand or at the time of a visit by one of the various inspection teams who have the duty of enforcing regulation, nothing else needs to be done. For auditors, insolvency practitioners and those who wish to be authorized to provide training places for either students or newly qualified members seeking practising certificates, there is a need to fulfil the CPD requirement to avoid the risk of losing their authorized status. Compliance is only tested, however, if they receive an inspection visit, or are asked to submit their CPD records for some other reason.

Compliance

After the initial unworkable attempts to fully police the system through the accreditation process, and full annual returns of CPD, the regime for ensuring compliance has subsequently relied heavily on the professional conscience of the membership, first through a gentle system of self-certification and now with no certification at all. In addition, over this period other changes have occurred in the way the profession operates which give additional sanctions against those who fail to comply with the CPD requirements. The first of these was the introduction of a system for authorizing those offices which wished to train students. Compliance with CPD requirements became mandatory for those wishing to be responsible for the training of students of the Institute. Next came the requirement to be registered if a member wanted to conduct investment business, audits or insolvency work. Again the relevant authorization or licence could be withheld in the event of failure to comply with the CPD requirements.

All of these developments have brought with them the necessity for members to submit to periodic inspection visits during which CPD records are usually examined.

It is difficult to see how the system could be policed more effectively without a major increase in the number of inspection teams which would, of course, involve costs which neither the profession nor its clients would particularly wish to bear. In any event, it is difficult to see the point in devoting resources to enforcing compliance when the second problem, the much more subtle question of relevance, has not yet been properly addressed.

Over the past 16 years or so ICAEW has tried it all and it is interesting that the Law Society seems to be going through the same learning curve at the moment, if rather more rapidly. It would seem from this that the ICAEW has learned over this period that there is a balance to be struck between being seen to be operating some control over members' CPD and the practicalities of actually doing something effective. The regime has gradually relaxed in its formal aspects while maintaining a commitment to CPD. But the conclusion which has to be drawn is that enforcing compliance with a CPD policy is not the real problem. As we have already suggested, professionals ought to be self-motivated anyway. The question which I wish to raise, therefore, is does this sort of a points and quota regime really achieve the object of the exercise, which is the maintenance of standards of professional competence?

Relevance – the real problem

The client requires competent advice in return for a reasonable fee. Any mechanism for maintaining professional standards, including CPD, must be devoted towards ensuring competence amongst the members of the professional body. It follows from this that a valid CPD system should, in addition to ensuring that professionals do something towards continuing the educational process after passing the professional exams, also direct them towards training which is useful in improving the level of service received by clients.

Unfortunately life is not quite that simple. Imagine a client looking for advice from an accountant about a technical issue – perhaps a tax problem has arisen. He may not realize it but he is probably faced with a choice from three types of adviser which we will call, in ascending order of cost, the novice, the practitioner, and the guru. Let us look in more detail at what happens when the client visits each of these advisers in turn.

The client visits a guru

In visiting a guru, the client has access to an expert in his or her specialization. The guru has spent many years acquiring this expertise which may be in a relatively limited field, and will have encountered most of the possible problems in this area.

The fees charged by the guru per hour of advice are likely to be high to fund the research required to maintain this degree of expertise and because the number of calls on the guru's time may be limited.

Unless the problem is extremely complex, it might have been possible for the client to visit someone with less expertise, who charges less, and still receive competent advice. Another way of looking at this would be to say that the amount of CPD undertaken which brought the guru to a level of expertise in excess of the client's needs is, for that client, wasted and therefore irrelevant.

The client visits a novice

In this case the level of fees is likely to be less per hour, but the client is likely to have to pay for at least some of the time spent by the novice in learning how to solve the problem. The client is paying for the novice's ability to acquire knowledge rather than the prior possession of that knowledge.

It may be that the client receives competent advice at a reasonable cost and is in no danger from this approach to the problem. Usually, however, client safety and professional ethics demand that the novice should be supervised.

The client visits a practitioner

Here the client should expect to pay a moderate fee in between the hourly rates of guru and novice. The client is paying for experience and a certain level of technical expertise. The practitioner should also be able to judge and to advise the client when the particular problem, or certain aspects of it, exceeds his level of competence. At this point a guru will be consulted.

Conclusion – client needs

Sometimes the client will need a guru, but often he will not. Novices need training (including CPD) to become practitioners. Some novices may go on to become gurus in due course. If the client needs a practitioner but gets a guru, the training from practitioner to guru will have been wasted. The client may not necessarily suffer by visiting a novice

Conclusion – CPD systems

A good CPD system will encourage the professional to achieve and maintain competence to serve the needs of the client. Thus if he holds himself out to be a guru, he will need and should receive credit for CPD which gives a high level of technical knowledge. The practitioner will have different requirements – greater breadth as opposed to depth – and a need for management, interpersonal and commercial skills in excess of the needs of the guru. A CPD system should encourage the proper assessment of these needs and give credit for training which meets those needs.

FOR AN ACCOUNTANT, WHAT WOULD BE RELEVANT CPD?

Five elements in training/competence

Just as we can see that the client may need to consult different practitioners with different mixes of skills, we can see that any practitioner needs to acquire a variety of different competences in order to serve his or her clientele effectively. An effective CPD system should encourage the acquisition of all of these different competences in an appropriate mix. I think of the various categories of knowledge and skills required as being defined as follows:

- *technical skills* – the ability to perform tasks required by professional duties
- *technical knowledge* – knowing the facts and information required by law or expected by clients
- *interpersonal skills* – the ability to deal with others eg, selling, presentation, influencing and negotiating skills
- *management skills* – managing self and others so that business objectives are met
- *commercial skills* – the skills required to run a profitable business.

Most new entrants to the profession are graduates, but there is no requirement for any relevant previous educational or work-based experience. The profession therefore has taken the decision to train its own from scratch. What is more it does this really quite quickly – from no knowledge/experience to practising certificate within, potentially, five years, although the typical time taken to become a partner in a firm of accountants is something more like ten years. In that time the trainee has to acquire all the different pieces to fit into the educational jigsaw for them to become competent to advise the public.

Four Stages of Career Development

Although these different elements of competence all need to be acquired before the accountant really becomes a fully fledged professional adviser – at least one major firm has plotted all the specific competences it requires from its people before they are regarded as being fit to be appointed partners – a firm's business practices will dictate that their acquisition will be phased in over time, with the emphasis on different skills at various points in the career.

I think of accountants as passing through four broad stages of development as their careers progress and the demands are such that the mix of training for the various types of skill and knowledge should be different in each phase. The four phases are as follows:

- *trainee* – the period from entry into the profession to passing the professional examinations – between three and five years
- *junior manager* – the period from qualification to practising certificate – about a further two years
- *senior manager* – the pre-partner phase, about a further four to eight years.
- *partner* – thereafter, although there are differing grades of partner.

These timescales are only given as an example and would be flexible depending on the abilities of the people concerned and the needs/policies of the firm.

The accountant will need to acquire the core technical skills and knowledge during the trainee phase. This core can be learned comparatively quickly, and simply enables the trainee to function in his or her job at a fairly rudimentary level. The trainee then moves on to acquire additional knowledge which is dictated by the examination syllabus and which is supposed to ensure a good coverage of the sort of things the 'typical' accountant needs to know. Not all this knowledge needs to be held by all accountants, however, and the requirements change as an individual's career progresses. Skills training is usually omitted from the process at this stage, perhaps because it is much easier to assess knowledge than it is to assess competence in skills. The end of the trainee phase marks the point where the CPD process begins.

It is during the junior manager phase that accountants really need to acquire the management and interpersonal skills which will enable them to become fully fledged professional advisers. Prior to this there simply has not been enough time. During this phase, accountants being professional advisers, it is also necessary to start to acquire some specific areas of technical expertise. This will normally be determined either by the areas in which the trainee showed particular aptitude during the training period or else dictated by specific client needs. There is therefore a good deal of pressure on the junior manager to acquire a large volume of new knowledge and skills.

During the senior manager phase the accountant has to prepare for the management of the practice itself and for becoming a principal in the business. The emphasis therefore shifts still further away from the need for technical knowledge towards more advanced management and commercial skills.

The final phase is the junior partner stage, where the person now has a stake in the equity of the business and is learning about owning and managing a business for real. Learning obviously does not stop just because you have reached the top table. Clients still expect informed advice although often pure technical expertise can be delegated to more junior members of the firm. Management problems and decisions, however, are becoming increasingly tricky – team-building, partnership disagreements, promotions to and within the partnership, mergers and acquisition – it is a wonder that the partner in practice ever has time for clients at all.

Figure 4.1 represents my suggestion of how the emphasis on the five types of knowledge/skill changes as an accountant's career progresses through its four stages. The precise percentages are not important, will differ from individual to individual and role to role and could never be proved objectively anyway. My belief is that the need for technical skills and technical knowledge training is heaviest in the early years and that this is replaced by a need for interpersonal, management and commercial skills training as the individual's career progresses.

Figure 4.2 shows how I estimate many accountants allocate their CPD effort in the post-qualifying years. Again the precise percentages are not important, but there is a strong tendency to attend technical knowledge-based courses rather than those dealing with the skills which are really required.

The role of the CPD system

A CPD system should recognize that in order to serve the needs of the client effectively, the post-qualification training needs of the individual practitioner will change in line with the different mix of skills which are demanded as his or her career progresses. It should therefore help to support and encourage the practitioner where CPD is undertaken fulfilling the practitioner's business needs which are in turn dictated by his or her clients. A

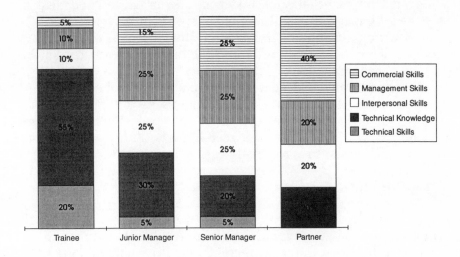

Figure 4.1 *Training needs model*

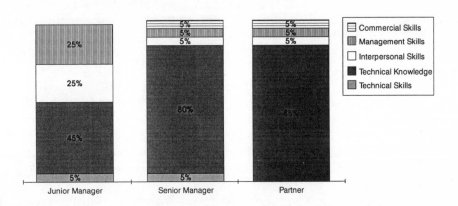

Figure 4.2 *Likely actual CPD*

system which is based purely on points or hours of course attendance is unlikely to provide this support and encouragement. Indeed I believe that such a system encourages a good deal of wasted effort on CPD. This is not because such a system is inherently wrong but it tends to have this effect because of the nature of courses which are on offer and the business pressures felt by today's professional.

The operation of CPD based on points or hours of course attendance tends to encourage practitioners to attend technical knowledge-based courses, often to the exclusion of all else, when, as we have seen, the real need is shifting away from knowledge-based towards skill-based training.

Hughes' Theory of Least Irrelevance

How it works is as follows: the busy practitioner – we will call him Walter, for reasons which will shortly become apparent – is seated at his desk. Enter his secretary bearing a cup of coffee, the indigestion tablets and the post which today includes the latest course catalogue from a major training provider. 'Oh help!' says the busy practitioner, 'I haven't done any CPD this year yet.' He takes a slurp of coffee and an indigestion tablet and looks through the course catalogue. 'Mildred', he says, 'book me on the VAT update, The Finance Act and the Accounting Standards update and that should sort the problem for another year.' His secretary might point out that these were the same three courses he has been on for the last five years and would it not be sensible to book them in advance in future, but she probably knows better than to do this and does not want to further disrupt his already disturbed digestive system.

Hughes' theory of least irrelevance states that the busy practitioner, being too busy to plan in advance what training is needed by himself and his staff, will select from any given course catalogue those courses which sound the least irrelevant to his work. As a result, although the demands of his Institute's CPD requirements are met in full, the benefits in terms of the service to be provided to his clients and his own professional development are minimal. What he should be doing is to seek out specific training which meets the firm's specific training needs.

The question must be therefore, 'How helpful are CPD requirements when expressed in terms of points or a number of hours attendance on courses?' The answer, for me, conjures up visions of many accountant and lawyer horses being led to the CPD water and drinking only in the most perfunctory manner, if at all. Maybe it should be, 'You can feed a course to Walter, but you can't make him think.'

Obviously CPD requirements serve some purpose because, on the most minimalist of levels, where a practitioner might do no CPD whatsoever, and be a genuine danger to the public, there is at least some exposure to an updating process. But these are the lost souls of the CPD cause and the benefit of the courses they attend is probably marginal. The good guys care enough and go on courses dictated by their genuine professional needs, and would do so with or without CPD requirements. The ones in the middle, the majority, probably including Walter, are usually not a danger to their clients, do their homework and their technical reading and regard CPD as an intrusion, when they could be benefiting so much more from the system. It might be thought that, for an accountant, attendance at almost any course on taxation, or the impact of company law changes on a company's year-end accounts, would always be good for the CPD record. But how many VAT updates does a good accountant need? Sometimes the experienced general practitioner could tell the lecturer a thing or two about his subject. If they cannot, some other member of the practice usually can.

In consequence, although there is some benefit from such courses, often much greater benefit from the same outlay of time and money would be derived from training in the other areas. Often the client expects the senior member of the firm not to be a guru, but to have the kind of experience which gives understanding of the way the world works, to be able to draw on that experience, to be able to come up with original and pertinent solutions to the problem at hand, and to be able to express his or her thoughts effectively.

So where does this leave the official CPD requirement? If those who really need it tend not to respond to the treatment, and the good guys will do it anyway and therefore don't need it, and the chaps in the middle, who might benefit from it are going on the wrong courses, why not abandon the whole thing?

SUGGESTED SYSTEM

As we have seen, a CPD policy is necessary, partly because the professional body needs to be seen to be doing something and partly because it does provide a stick with which to beat those who are failing in their professional duty and might be a danger to the public. There must, however, be a better way.

My thesis is that, instead of insisting on a rigid quota of hours or points, the professional body should require that its members in practice should, on a regular, but not necessarily frequent basis:

- draw up a strategic training plan covering the competences required from all grades of staff.

At least annually they should:

- review performance against this plan for themselves and their staff
- determine the training action required in the forthcoming year to meet the needs disclosed by the review
- set a budget so that resources are available for the action plan to be carried out
- monitor performance against the action plan for the past year so that shortfalls can be made up.

I fully expect that this process would reveal the need for an increased training budget for those in the junior manager phase. I also am confident, however, that both this increased level of expenditure and the opportunity cost of the planning process, will be more than compensated for by the reduction in wasted training time spent by more senior and therefore more expensive managers and partners and by the increased productivity of well-trained staff.

The ICAEW experience shows that there is no need to force practitioners to submit their plans and evidence of the review process to the professional body for checking. This serves no practical purpose and only leads to disgruntlement amongst the membership. The periodic inspection visits for practice regulation purposes are all that is required to enforce the message.

The final advantage is that, provided the new system is communicated well to the membership, the professional body will be seen as supporting the members' needs, rather than imposing still more regulation on them from on high and this will improve its standing in the eyes of its members.

CONCLUSIONS

A CPD policy plays a necessary part in reinforcing the credibility of a professional body if it is to sustain the dual role of trade association and regulator of standards.

The usual type of CPD system operated by professional bodies, based on a quota of points and hours, is not effective in ensuring that members obtain CPD which is relevant to the needs of the clients they serve. A much better system would focus on the assessment of training needs, the development of training plans and the monitoring of compliance with those plans.

5

Continuing Professional Development in Engineering

Chris Senior

CONTEXT

Continuing Professional Development (CPD) is not a new activity for engineers. In the 19th century the great engineers Brunel and Stephenson had to develop many new skills in building the railways. Technical, managerial and, not least, political skills were crucial in pioneering new frontiers. Similar challenges face engineers today in developing new products and services and in tackling new markets. The difference lies in the pace of the changes taking place and in their variety. The half life of technology has decreased from decades to years; in information technology it is measured in months. Much of the technology which will be in use in ten years' time has not yet been invented.

At the same time the business environment is changing, as companies operate internationally in complex and highly competitive markets. Technology can be transferred around the world to make use of low labour costs and the availability of skilled and flexible staff. Design services may be separated from manufacturing; both may be carried out close to the customer and on his or her terms. The timescale from concept to delivery is counted in weeks or months rather than years. This applies in all branches of engineering. The interactive compact disc, the latest vehicle the aeroplane, and the video telephone are examples of complex and innovative products delivered in an astonishingly short time to meet demanding markets.

As well as changes to the technology and markets there are profound changes to the structure of the industries which engineers serve. Employers are having to focus on a number of, often conflicting, demands. These include the need for high quality products and services, increased speed of delivery, and flexibility of operations. Their responses are to decrease staff numbers, to subcontract services and production, to develop flatter organizational structures and work units which are flexible, accountable and customer-focused. Failure to adapt, eg, in shipbuilding, has dire consequences. However, in telecommunications, motor manufacturing, steel production, materials technology, and much of construction, UK employers have adapted and retained their high world reputation. Many medium and small companies provide quality products and services. It is essential that all employers continue to improve, year by year, so as to survive and succeed in a world market where competition continually increases.

These changes impact on engineering staff in a number of significant ways. A prime consequence is that engineers need to continually adapt their mix of competences to meet the changing requirements of their employers and clients. With changes in technology they need to update their technical knowledge both in their own and in other specialisms. Since most engineering projects require a mix of technologies, engineers must acquire an awareness of related subject areas. All engineers need skills in information technology. In the UK the relative specialism of engineers in their initial education and training emphasizes the requirement for broadening their technological base.

Success as an engineer depends more than ever on a combination of technical know-how, managerial skills, commercial awareness and personal effectiveness. Initial education focuses on the first of these. Professional development needs continually to build up a portfolio of competences focusing on the latter areas. Engineers usually work in multi-disciplinary projects which require communication and team-working skills. Above all, products and services must always be commercially viable. Engineers must act as business engineers. This need was highlighted in a report from The Engineering Council (1988) entitled *Management and Business Skills for Engineers*.

The employment market for engineering staff is changing rapidly. No longer are they likely to work for a single, probably large, employer for most of their career. A series of jobs with different employers is becoming common. There will be changes in direction and breaks in a career, for a variety of reasons. As a result, engineers must manage their career development, regularly assessing themselves against the needs of the market. They must cope with uncertainty. They have to be proactive in seeking out opportunities for improvement and learning. Above all, engineers must own their CPD and act in partnership with, rather than be dependent upon, their employers and other organizations.

CPD, as part of lifelong learning, is aimed at enabling professionals to respond to change. Much of the action currently taking place is a reaction to the need for technical updating, management development and business survival. Important as these are, CPD has a wider role. It aims to enhance the potential of all engineers by encouraging innovation and enterprise. The challenge for CPD is not just to help engineers and their employers to adapt to change but to be a driving force for change.

In engineering there has been a long tradition of professional development based on an engineering degree followed by training and responsible experience. Standards for education and training have been established over many years by the professional engineering institutions, coordinated by The Engineering Council. The institutions have traditionally been involved in CPD through their learned society activities. This includes the provision of meetings, courses and conferences, and the publication of journals and books. In 1985 The Engineering Council published *A Call to Action* which indicated that a more structured approach was required. In particular it highlighted the roles of the four key partners in CPD as individual engineers and technicians, employers, professional institutions, and providers of CPD courses and learning material. A pilot project was carried out and subsequently a policy statement, *National System; Framework for Action* was published in 1991. Action is underway to implement this. This has three essential strategies:

- promotion of understanding of CPD
- setting standards for CPD
- supporting action on CPD.

PROMOTION OF CPD

All the partners in CPD need to understand what CPD is, why it is important, and how they can best contribute.

CPD is defined by the CPD in Construction Group as

> The systematic maintenance, improvement and broadening of knowledge and skill, and the development of personal

qualities necessary for the execution of professional and technical duties throughout the practitioner's working life.

The Engineering Council promotes the term Continuing Professional Development to emphasize:

- the responsibility of engineers for continuous improvement and development to ensure high competence as professionals throughout their career
- the need for development to include a range of technical, commercial, financial and management subjects
- the use of a wide range of structured job-related activities including courses, distance learning, in-company programmes, professional institution meetings, and research.

The Council holds meetings with and gives presentations to all the partners. An annual conference, sponsored with other professional bodies outside engineering, is administered by CRAC, the Careers Research and Advisory Council, with support from the Department for Employment.

A CPD promotion document *The Practical Guide to Good Practice* was published by the Council in 1992. In response to demand, a regular eight-page newsletter *CPD Link* is produced three times each year. This provides news on CPD developments, promotes examples of good practice and raises important issues.

Most of the professional institutions include articles on CPD in their journals and hold meetings to debate CPD. A number produce guidance and information documents. Promotion and sharing of experience is helped by the existence of the CPD in Construction Group, and the Engineering CPD Forum. These provide opportunities for sharing information and for discussion of key issues, and act as focal points for joint action.

Setting Standards

High standards for education and training are a key feature of the engineering profession, providing essential benchmarks for both members and users of engineering services. In the past, the focus has been on requirements for initial qualifications. In the future, this must also include criteria for continued recognition as a professional engineer through requirements for CPD. Agreed standards for CPD will help individual engineers and their employers to know what is expected of them and underpin the activities of the institutions. It will also provide evidence of commitment by the profession to continued high standards of competence.

The Engineering Council and the professional institutions have established a framework of standards for CPD. This specifies the responsibilities of the professional institutions for setting standards for their members, as detailed in a Code of Practice for CPD, and for providing support to their members to meet the standards. This Framework and Code should be seen as an essential part of the quality assurance system for the profession.

The code of practice for CPD places an obligation on members to:

- *Manage their CPD.* CPD is not an end in itself, but an investment. To achieve results, it must be planned through a process of identifying development needs, recognizing learning opportunities and taking appropriate action. Usually this must be done in partnership with an employer.
- *Record CPD achievements.* Investment in CPD requires a regular audit of activities and results. Professionals will increasingly be expected to provide evidence of continued learning and competence. In the future this evidence is likely to make use of the national framework of occupational standards and vocational qualifications.
- *Support the learning of others.* Just as engineers do not work best on their own, neither do they learn best on their own. As professionals, engineers have a responsibility to support other staff in the process of continual improvement. Coaching and mentoring are key skills for all senior engineers.

The code should operate from January 1996. It does not aim to control or prescribe what engineers should do, since individuals have unique needs and opportunities. It does aim to encourage engineers, as professionals, to be committed to a process of continual learning.

Many institutions place a general obligation on their members to keep up to date. Specific requirements are laid down by some institutions with several expecting their members to carry out a minimum amount of CPD. For example, members of the Institution of Civil Engineers are expected to achieve five days of CPD a year as requirement for Fellowship. The Institution of Mechanical Engineers expects members to undertake a minimum of 50 hours CPD activities each year. To increase recognition of CPD the Institution of Electrical Engineers has launched a voluntary scheme based on professional development points for approved CPD activities. These schemes are seen as obligatory for their members. No institution has yet produced a mandatory system.

National Education and Training targets for the UK have been established by the CBI and promoted by the government through TECs/LECs. CPD relates to the lifelong learning targets in two ways. The CPD Code of Practice is a response to the requirement that by 1996 all employees should take part in training and development activities. In the case of employers The Engineering Council supports the Investors in People standard. A joint statement indicates that CPD and IIP are complementary since both focus on continuous improvements to work performance.

Supporting Action

There is evidence that the majority of engineers and their employers recognize the need for CPD. However, there is less understanding of how best to take action to achieve real benefits. A survey showed that over 70 per cent of engineers were involved in CPD. Most of them indicated that there was scope for improvement in their CPD; only 25 per cent were assessing their needs and planning action in a structured way.

In its policy statement The Engineering Council proposed a framework within which action should be taken to progress CPD. This showed that the key partnership for learning should be between individual engineers and their employers. Structured CPD activities should complement learning through work experience and be planned so that CPD contributes to corporate performance and individual career development. CPD should be treated as an investment and be managed to achieve real benefits.

In managing CPD, engineers should analyse their development needs taking into account:

- an assessment of experience and competences
- their career intentions, short- and long-term
- the requirements of their professional institutions
- relevant personal interests
- immediate work demands.

Individual action plans should be developed and be realistic. Engineers need to discuss ideas with their employer if possible and take note of guidance from relevant professional bodies.

The CPD activities chosen will vary and depend on a number of factors. These include the particular learning objectives, the cost-effectiveness of different activities, and the preferred learning styles of the individual. Development activities should include a variety of approaches:

- courses (in-company and external)
- distance and open learning programmes
- structured reading/self-study assignments
- professional institution meetings/activities
- coaching/tutoring/teaching
- making presentations
- writing papers and articles for publication
- seminars/conferences/exhibitions
- secondments/special projects
- relevant voluntary work.

Employers have a key role to assist individual engineers in analysing needs and implementing plans. This may be through a structured appraisal or development system. However, the most critical factor is for managers and senior engineers to encourage their staff to continually develop their competence and to do this within the culture of a learning organization. There should be an implicit learning contract between individuals committed to their continued learning and the organization providing support for this learning.

Support for this core partnership can be provided by professional institutions and providers of CPD. Institutions have key roles in challenging their members to manage their CPD, to assist them in identifying CPD needs and learning opportunities and in implementing their CPD. Planning documents are provided by a number of institutions; The Engineering Council publishes the *Career Manager*. These aim to help engineers audit their experience, examine CPD needs, plan appropriate action and record learning achievements.

An important requirement is for engineers to own their CPD, to seek out opportunities for learning and to increase their demand for CPD. Workshops have been piloted to assist engineers with this process. The Engineering Council is establishing these in the regions and examining possible sources of distance learning material.

Studies of the CPD needs of engineers indicate that there is a clear requirement for guidance and information covering a variety of subjects. Individuals need help to know what options are available in terms of courses, conferences, distance learning material and other less formal methods. Sources of funding and other advice is needed. Professional institutions can provide advice and information, and link with national and international sources including relevant databases.

The focus for support to engineers and employers is increasingly through regional staff. The Engineering Council has found that regional activities have great potential for providing information and advice, carrying out surveys and coordinating the provision of courses and meetings. Professional development centres are being established to give guidance and to encourage the local provision of CPD programmes and learned society activities; this may include assessments of competence towards vocational and professional qualifications. A key strategy is to link with other relevant regional initiatives and organizations to ensure effective partnership and joint action.

RECOGNITION AND MEASUREMENT

The ultimate pay-off for CPD should be long-term employability and success in an engineer's career. Any systems for recognizing CPD should support this central aim. However, there would be value in engineers and employers positioning CPD within a national and international framework of requirements and qualifications. This would increase motivation for CPD and provide some confidence that learning may be transferable and recognized by other partners.

There are attempts by several professional institutions to establish systems based essentially on a required minimum number of points for 'accredited' CPD activities. These focus on measuring CPD activity in terms of time, rather than the learning outcome, and give emphasis to formal courses rather than the essential on-the-job development. A more sustainable approach must focus on measuring the learning outcomes in some way. This may be through a system of credit units which would be defined in terms of content and level, with specified means of assessment. Individuals would be able to use these credits towards academic and professional qualifications. Experience of the Open University and of the Credit Accumulation and Transfer Scheme indicate that an overall framework for credit could be established. A working group has identified key requirements for a European-based credit system based on using records of achievement.

The Engineering Council is leading a major review of engineering formation taking into account the changing needs of employers for engineering skills, and increasing requirements for flexible and broad-based engineers. A key requirement is for engineers to build up and maintain their professional qualification through a continuous process of development. Assessed units of competence would be the key building blocks, and could be the basis for required CPD.

Postgraduate programmes increasingly reflect the market needs for them to be modular, part-time, work-related, using a variety of learning methods and including a combination of commercial and managerial subjects. Examples of this are the Integrated Graduate Development Schemes, of which there are over 24 in the UK, providing close partnership between universities and employers. In addition a masters degree in technology management has been established by a consortium of universities, providing an opportunity for flexible, quality provision, building on the strengths of the members.

There is considerable interest in CPD and continuing education of engineers throughout the world. In Europe SEFI (Société Européenne pour la Formation des Ingenieurs) has several working groups examining key issues. FEANI (Fédération Européenne d'Associations Nationales d'Ingenieurs) has a CPD commission which is examining systems for quality assurance for providers of continuing education. The possibility of some CPD requirements for the European Engineer qualification is being considered. IACEE (International Association of Continuing Engineering Education) is active in promoting continuing education through publications and conferences. The UK engineering profession takes an active part in these organizations and in the development of innovative international programmes. Through The Engineering Council there are links with, and contributions to, CPD activities in other professions both in the UK and overseas.

A report, *Lifelong Learning of Engineers in Industry* (Otala, 1993) highlights the practices in Europe, the USA and Japan. The international nature of industry and technology leads all countries to treat continuing education of engineers as a priority. However, different approaches are being taken. In Japan there is a focus on company activities with on-the-job learning integrated with the business. In the USA the individual engineer is a major driving force with an emphasis on treating training as an investment with measurable return. A difficulty in all countries is promoting learning in smaller companies. There is a common focus on competence being an asset of an individual; the career plan is becoming a competence development plan.

CONCLUSIONS

CPD is high on the agenda of the engineering profession. There is recognition that engineers can no longer rely on their initial education and training to equip them for their entire working life. Sustained professional competence requires continual attention to CPD both by individual engineers and employers, supported by professional and academic institutions.

The focus has moved from identifying the need for CPD to increasing the commitment to and demand for CPD, and to providing support so that effective action is taken. There is general consensus on the standards required for CPD (five days/year, variety of learning methods, evidence of planning and learning achievements). However, important issues such as recognition of CPD, monitoring and measurement, quality control and international standards, need to be examined and will provide opportunities for much debate and possible initiatives.

CPD has a number of central roles but there is potential tension between several important objectives. On the one hand CPD is a mechanism for helping engineers to respond positively to changing technical and commercial requirements in the market. As part of the change process CPD must be ambitious with a focus on innovation and enterprise. Engineers must be encouraged and motivated to view CPD as an investment in their future and that of their employer. They must own CPD and adapt it to their own needs and opportunities. On the other hand, CPD can be a mechanism for providing evidence of continuing professional competence. Standards of professionalism are determined by national and international bodies with their tendency to prescribe, measure and control. The driving force can become the need to meet the minimum requirements for membership of a professional body.

The challenge is to establish strategies for CPD which motivate engineers to continually improve their competence and their contribution to business performance. This is most likely to take place when engineers act as professionals by owning their CPD and acting with the grain of their own jobs and learning styles. The profession should expect its members to provide evidence of their learning. The framework of guidance, regional activities, standards and competence measures is being established to support this process. CPD must continue to be a central force to ensure that engineers provide leadership in the industries they serve.

REFERENCES

The Engineering Council (1985) *A Call to Action*, The Engineering Council, London

The Engineering Council (1988) *Management and Business Skills for Engineers*, The Engineering Council, London.

The Engineering Council (1991) *National System; Framework for Action*, The Engineering Council, London.

The Engineering Council (1992) reprinted 1994 *The Practical Guide to Good Practice*, The Engineering Council, London.

Otala, L (1993) *Lifelong Learning of Engineers in Industry*, IACEE report, International Association for Continuing Engineering Education, Helsinki

6

Continuing Professional Development at British Rail

Graham Taylor

INTRODUCTION

This chapter describes the development of a CPD scheme for British Rail Maintenance Ltd (BRML), its planning, implementation and current position. British Rail has, of course, been a major employer of professionals, particularly in engineering but also in related professions. Each professional is accountable to their own professional body for their CPD and this scheme shows how CPD is integrated into the HRD activity of this major employer.

FIRST STEPS

Until 1987, BRML Training and Development was based upon traditional BR concepts which had provided well for the core needs of management while BR was a public sector organization. It then became a holding company which had to operate and compete with both the BR operating business and the private sector as a stand-alone business for the first time. As a consequence of this development there was a considerable need for change.

The old railway culture which extended back 150 years to the origins of the railways had to be replaced by an injection of modern management. This meant either recruiting new people or developing the existing group of experienced professionals. They chose the latter course.

The chairman commissioned a senior management development programme to identify solutions and ways forward. An external management consultant team was contracted to develop and deliver the programme and this proved beneficial in setting the foundations for ongoing development. A further need was identified to develop a greater degree of professional standing of management staff and for them to be more responsible for identifying and taking ownership of their own training and development needs.

At that time, the BR chairman was involved with the engineering professional institutions in the redevelopment of the Engineering Graduate Training Scheme to improve standards and was introduced to the concept of Continuing Professional Development (CPD). Proposals were put to the BRML board, which were accepted, and objectives set for the introduction of CPD.

Preparation

With no knowledge or experience of CPD, support was necessary. Another British Rail business had also started on the CPD trail and had contracted a firm of consultants to design and support their implementation plan. This group was approached and contracted to induct all BRML management on the concepts of CPD, and to conduct initial interviews in establishing personal development plans. It was agreed that I would work with the consultant and eventually take over responsibility for the CPD scheme.

The decision to begin with management staff was taken for two reasons: first, CPD had been identified as a management development need and second, CPD could be integrated with managers' annual performance reviews.

Following discussions with the consultant the implementation plan was developed for all seven BRML sites which are geographically spread between Southampton and Glasgow. The agreed plan was:

- briefing of depot managers and their senior managers on CPD concepts, methods and benefits
- briefing of all management staff, concluding with personal development analysis project sheets
- interviews with managers concluding with agreement and recording of training and development needs
- compilation of depot and group training and development plans.

From this process a problem emerged over how to convince

senior management of probable benefits. A number of concerns were expressed which suggested that unless individual managers were prepared to accept ownership there would be a high drop-out rate. In the event, the CPD induction programme, which was modelled on The Engineering Council's CPD vision statement, created the commitment needed.

Implementation

CPD Induction Programme

The aim was to create:

> a company whose people are the most skilled in the railway industry, who are highly developed throughout their career and are professionally, technically and managerially competent.

Objectives for the induction programme were established:

- the concepts and principles of CPD
- why CPD is needed
- the benefits to business and the individual
- how CPD is to be introduced
- professional and personal development
- the four-way partnership:
  - the manager
  - the employer
  - the professional institutions
  - the providers
- introduction to personal development plans.

The level of interest generated was higher than expected. There were some reservations and doubts expressed, mainly about factors such as commitment by the company, lack of time, uncertainty about job security and career advancement. Some considered that the main objective was to have all managers gain membership of their respective professional body. However, once the link between CPD and managing the business through the development of its professionals was made clear, these difficulties disappeared.

Each manager emerged from the CPD induction with a personal review form to complete, the purpose of which was to identify:

- where they were in their career
- how effective they were at their job

- how they could move forward.

Four areas were examined:

- present job
- future roles
- professional and personal development
- key development plan.

One-to-one interviews were held with the consultant to review the completed forms and identify not only the training and development needs but to iron out any issues relating to the role of the professional bodies and CPD within the business.

On completion of all the interviews the consultant and I had established training and development needs and grouped them as a) those common to all depots and b) individual needs. Additionally, under the heading 'professional recognition', managers registered their interest in additional educational and professional qualifications. It was agreed that all identified training and development needs established from performance reviews would be included with CPD training plans. This approach meant that there was an integration of professional development with the job and business requirements.

A development plan was formulated for each manager and I presented a report on progress to the management board in which I highlighted certain difficulties and obstacles which needed to be managed. These included:

- not all needs had been identified
- not all action plans were complete
- methods being implemented were primarily course-based
- lack of personal ownership of development plans
- need to support managers.

The management board considered that the underlying key factor to address was ownership, for unless the individual manager was committed to their own professional development needs the scheme would fail. It was decided that training officers would act as facilitators to discuss development plans with individual managers in order to enhance the concepts of CPD, highlight its value and benefits and emphasize its nature as a continuing process, not a 'one-off'. Methods of taking individual ownership of the programme focused upon leaving the individual to review their own progress with follow-up sessions with training officers continuing in their role as facilitators providing support and monitoring progress.

REVIEW AND ASSESSMENT

In March 1994 the programme had been in place for 18 months and a report was presented to the BRML executive assessing the level of achievement of the 1993 development plans. The report highlighted the following:

- training and development needs met ranged from 25 to 80 per cent
- methods still centred too much upon attendance at training courses
- managers were keeping themselves updated but there was a need to broaden horizons
- professional recognition: those involved were very committed and making good progress
- difficulty in maintaining and updating personal development plans
- ownership: improvement not consistent
- need to give greater consideration to training and development at performance review interviews.

Identifying the Gaps

A complete review of the effectiveness of the CPD project was needed to identify objectives and approaches for the next steps. Investigation of CPD projects both inside and outside the rail industry established that continuing professional development was mainly promoted not under the the CPD title but incorporated into personal development plans with CPD principles and methods being used.

Problems experienced by BRML in implementation were common and we were not alone in failing to gain everyone's acceptance of ownership for self-development. Facilitation was needed to maintain progress, as was continuous assurance that CPD was alive and well and succeeding. The review showed significant gaps that needed to be filled. The most significant were:

- to broaden personal development plans which were directed too much to job training
- to include company needs more
- to extend learning methods
- to integrate performance reviews with personal development plans

- PDPs to be more balanced and include long- and short-term goals as well as projections
- to introduce a method for the individuals to log their needs, action plans, methods and achievements.

The next steps are to work closely with the training officers/facilitators on:

- inducting new people into the CPD process
- coaching in the formulation of individual development plans
- setting up systems to monitor progress
- establishing guidelines on methods of learning, meeting educational needs and professional career progression
- developing the facilitators as coaches/mentors
- developing new strategies to encourage ownership of self-development.

ACHIEVEMENTS/LESSONS LEARNT

At the start of CPD sound foundations were already in place. The company had achieved BS 5750 accreditation and was working towards ISO 9002; they were also committed to Investors in People. All managers had an annual performance review which identified any training and development needs.

So what was achieved by introducing CPD? It has provided the individual manager with the opportunity to:

- consider their current and future career and development needs
- formulate a personal development plan and take ownership
- broaden their learning and professional aspirations
- improve their capability in the management of change.

The cost/benefits for the company have not been calculated nor has the cost of implementation. However, as the training, development and professional needs of managers are met, job and business improvement will become increasingly apparent. The work currently underway has proved that CPD has to be managed to be effective for both the company and the individual and that requires a positive commitment from the board room and senior management.

So what has been learnt?

- CPD is about people, achieving through learning, training, education and about improving quality standards, products and services

- ownership is important, as is commitment by the employer
- results have to be earned; there are no measurable benefits overnight or without the investment of money and time
- implementation needs to be applied sensitively, systematically and convincingly
- individuals need mentors, coaches and records of progress
- senior management involvement and ownership are vital
- PDPs should include non work-related items

Benefits in business improvement and performance have outweighed any learning problems. By the time BRML/Level 5 Group hand over to new owners in the private sector, CPD will be established, with managers having accepted ownership for their personal development plans and measurable results being achieved and recognized.

7

Continuing Professional Development in Continental Europe

Anna Hughes

The management of CPD in continental Europe is simplified by the existence of a legal code which sets out the boundaries and requirements of professional conduct. This code usually includes an obligation to update and frequently specifies the body which will be responsible for ensuring that practitioners fulfil this part of their professional duty. In France and Germany, the professional associations are conferred with state power to facilitate the provision of CPD for their members. In some professions in Germany, universities and technical colleges are required by *Länd* (regional state) law to provide CPD courses.

In Germany, Denmark and France, the legal stipulation to provide CPD is extended to include national CPD incentives: German practitioners in all professions may offset the costs of participation in CPD against tax; Danish architects may negotiate a proportion of their salary to be paid into a training fund; similarly, French practitioners are required by law to contribute part of their earnings to a training fund. This background support facilitates the establishment of a CPD infrastructure with financial and administrative resources to provide CPD. The form this management infrastructure takes depends on the size of the country, its politics, and some practical considerations.

In Denmark and The Netherlands, both small countries, CPD tends to be organized centrally, and frequently there is one location at which courses are organized. Danish pharmacists and engineers both congregate at one location. In The Netherlands, most CPD has been taken over by *Stichting voor Post Academisch*

Onderwijs (private post-academic educational organizations) which organize courses in one subject area for the whole country.

By contrast, the political and federal structures of Germany and Spain require that education comes under the jurisdiction of the regional authorities. The *Länd* authorities in Germany and the Autonomous Communities in Spain are responsible for most aspects of education. In France, political changes at the state level in the 1980s meant that professional associations had to change their centralized CPD system to a devolved one.

There may be an advantage to giving management responsibility to smaller entities: practitioners in the larger *Länder* in Germany have not found it practical to attend courses after work because of the distances from the office to the course location. On the other hand, there are some small French regions which cannot afford to mount courses because of their small membership and resulting low income. There seems to be an optimum size for regions in managing CPD efficiently.

These structural aids to managing CPD can be enhanced by functional elements carried out by the bodies responsible for organizing CPD. The most important of these elements is efficient marketing. In Portugal, a moribund CPD system for pharmacists was revived in 1990 by the introduction, by the Association of Portuguese Pharmacists, of effective marketing techniques and targeted courses. The success of the management of this programme has been shown in the doubling of participation from 1990 to the present. In the same way, in Spain, the Technological University of Valencia, a provider of a high proportion of technological post-qualification courses, has increased its provision of short courses targeted at small and medium-sized enterprises (SMEs). Its action is in response to the demand for such courses from the region's SMEs which make up the majority of the Valencian market.

Another aspect of marketing is the creation of a niche activity. In France, another technological university, the University of Paris-Sud, offers courses only in high-tech electronic engineering, catering for the Parisian 'Silicon Valley' in which the university is located. Management and language courses are offered by other institutions.

The Danes have developed an effective tool to reduce the costs of offering courses in highly specialized subject-matter. The Danish Post-graduate Engineering Association (*DIEU*) has initiated the formation of consortia amongst engineering companies so that they will benefit from economies of scale in participating in these courses. Equally, *DIEU* saves its own resources by encouraging a greater number of participants in courses which are expensive to set up and run.

A number of professions have been considering the introduction of distance-learning materials in order to counteract the problem of non-attendance. The University of Paris-Sud already offers satellite-transmitted material and, again in France, notaries may use distance-learning material instead of attending courses.

How some professional associations and training organizations have established their management of CPD will now be discussed in a number of examples.

DANISH POST-GRADUATE ENGINEERING ASSOCIATION (DIEU)

Danish graduate associations are extremely effective providers of CPD, for a number of reasons. First, they are able constantly to recruit new members from present undergraduates, so they never lose contact with their members; second, they have sufficient resources to build their own purpose-built accommodation; and third, they operate in an efficient, market-driven way. The last point could be aided by the fact that they are not the professional associations and, as a result, can act in a more independent way.

DIEU was established in 1975 by the Danish Society of Chemical, Civil, Electrical and Mechanical Engineers and the Society of Engineers in Denmark to improve the status and market value of its members. Until recently, there were a number of other providers of Continuing Engineering Education (CEE) in Denmark, but the methods used by *DIEU* to market its products have proved so successful that the other providers no longer feature much in the market.

DIEU provides courses and seminars of varying lengths, from two hours to 33 days. It also offers company-tailored courses. Currently, the highest demand amongst engineers is for technology management and *DIEU* duly provides most of its courses in this field.

DIEU has monitored its participant profile since 1988 and instituted changes to take account of any shifts, illustrating the flexibility which is an essential element of its success. In 1988, most participants came to their first *DIEU* courses at the age of

28–30 years. They were interested only in technical subjects. In their next phase of training, they expected to concentrate on personal development of 'soft' courses. These were followed by general management courses and, subsequently, high-level technical management courses. By 1993, the entry profile had altered. Technology is changing so rapidly that engineering graduates need new knowledge as soon as they graduate. Accordingly, new graduates began to enrol on the highly specialized courses. At the same time, they needed general management courses. Demand, therefore, has been reversed and telescoped into highly intensive and wide-ranging courses.

NIEDERSACHSEN, GERMANY, *ARCHITEKTENKAMMER*

DIEU is an example of a centralized, private organization managing CPD; Niedersachsen's *Architektenkammer* (architectural chamber) offers an example of a professional association operating in a regionalized system.

The *Architektenkammern* are responsible by law for the delivery and assessment of CPD. Niedersachsen's architectural laws set out the task of the *Kammer*: 'to provide and nurture building methods, especially building design and the architect's special skills, and to provide professional education in all its forms.'

In order to fulfil its duty, the *Kammer* has established its own educational institution to offer CPD courses. Subject-matter for the courses is decided by the architects' parliament, which agrees proposals for a five-yearly programme, arranged in six-monthly themes. The *Kammer* then arranges seminars, trips and courses around these themes. Ecological considerations are now high priority among German architects and the course content reflects their concerns. The *Kammer* also makes use of Hannover University's Institute for Architecture and Planning Theory, thereby maintaining contact with up-to-date research.

NOTAIRES IN FRANCE

In a devolved power structure similar to Germany, one branch of the legal profession in France, the *notaires* (notaries), operates a decentralized system of managing its CPD. Practitioners are gathered into *Chambres de Notaires* (chambers) in their region and, at a regional level, into 31 *Conseils Régionales du Notariat* (regional councils). Both organizations arrange CPD for their members.

There are a number of other providers of CPD, including the *Conseil Supérieur du Notariat* in Paris, but most practitioners make use of their local providers and there is no central decree governing the content of courses or requiring attendance from practitioners.

The *Chambres de Notaires* organize short seminars for their members. Courses are likely to reflect local concerns: property, tax or family law. The *Conseils Régionales* organize annual seminars on general topics: GATT and the reorganization of agricultural business law; law of wine; and issues on European and international tax law have been past themes of these meetings.

French *notaires* benefit from a highly organized devolved system of managing their CPD. On the other hand, the infrastructure of the notarial profession works against the effective management of CPD. The essence of the profession is its availability to the local population: *notaires* are dispersed throughout the country. Some *notaires* are in partnership and can take the time to attend courses, but most are in single-person practices and are not able to do so. The *Conseil Supérieur* has responded to this difficulty by distributing distance-learning materials. This does not solve the problem entirely: the value of CPD, as acknowledged by the *Conseil Supérieur*, is the contact with other practitioners with similar difficulties and solutions to those difficulties.

CONCLUSIONS

Some of the management styles and solutions to problems are strikingly similar in these examples, and they could be taken as a blueprint for good management practice in CPD. They also illustrate the optimum use of the conditions in which the professions exist in those countries.

The effective management of CPD as illustrated in the examples includes a mix of structural support and functional support for CPD:

- a system well supported by legislation
- a proactive professional association using effective marketing techniques
- employers interested in and supportive of CPD
- a variety of outlets for CPD provision
- motivated practitioners.

These elements may be adapted to many professions and many contexts. There is no specific model, however, for the most effective CPD management. The degree of success in the management of CPD depends on a number of factors which will differ from profession to profession and from country to country. Whatever the prevailing régime, in order to progress, individual professions must adapt themselves to changes.

Note
This chapter is based on the research project carried out by Anna Hughes during 1993–4 for the University of Bristol and the Higher Education Funding Council for England. The work has been published as *Developing European Professions: Delivering Continuing Professional Development in Europe* (1994) University of Bristol.

8

Continuing Professional Development: Challenge and Change

Carol Dix

PROFESSIONAL BODIES AND CPD: THE BACKGROUND

Professional bodies in Britain have always upheld strong cultural and ethical standards that serve as a solid and dependable spine to the varied dimensions of our working lives.

In times of change, we are ever more dependent on the professional bodies to be one step ahead of the game in introducing new ideas, concepts and demands on their membership, so that those values and standards are maintained. In future years, employers will turn to the professional bodies for some form of leadership, just as we have learned to rely on them in decades past.

In May 1993, The Local Government Management Board published *Professional Development – Challenge and Change* to encourage the professional bodies in local government to meet the challenge of the move towards competence-based qualifications. The sister publication in 1994, *Continuing Professional Development – Partnership for Change* continued the debate by emphasizing the need for professional bodies, employers and members of professional bodies to establish effective partnerships in order to deliver quality assured continuing professional development. The aim of the publication was to encourage both professional bodies and local government employers to work together in a new form of partnership for the benefit of us all.

Change is all around us whether we work in the central and local government sectors, the private sector, or view the world as employer, education and training provider, student, professional or employee. The fact that each and every one of us must adapt

100

to change and new challenges has led to a certain amount of discomfort and insecurity. But the challenge that is presented to us as a nation – namely to produce a more competent workforce and one that will be more closely suited to the needs of a competitive society – should ultimately be stimulating and rewarding.

THE CHANGING ROLE OF THE PROFESSIONAL WITHIN LOCAL GOVERNMENT

Once a job with the local borough, county or district council – for the young solicitor, accountant, environmental health officer, architect, surveyor, planner, social worker or administrator – very likely meant a safe and secure career for life. But today the evolution of local authorities from their role as public servants to that of enabling authorities has made enormous changes in their attitudes as employers.

Professor John Stewart comments on new groupings of professionals within departments and the impact this can have on professional boundaries and dividing lines:

> Local authorities are witnessing changing organisational patterns. Indeed the traditional patterns are being challenged every day. New groupings of departments are now seen together: for example, architects, planners and engineers may now all work as one team.
>
> A housing department may be suddenly thrown into the contractor/client divide and require the in-house services of an accountant or solicitor. Protectorate bodies such as Environmental Health and Trading Standards may be forced to work in close co-operation, or even competitively. (LGMB, 1993).

What is the new professionalism?
- dynamic knowledge and skills with less emphasis on basic training, and more on a changing repertoire of knowledge and skill
- external focus – on the customer and client rather than on the profession
- adherence to the values of the local authority as well as the professional values, so that the new professionalism sustains rather than denies the diversity of local government
- authority given by those whom the profession serves rather than assumed by qualification alone. (Stewart, 1988)

LOCAL GOVERNMENT: A QUESTION OF PARTNERSHIPS

The local government employer has to work in partnership with requirements from central government for training and development; with recommendations from the professional bodies for the updating of their members; with their own financially imposed restraints; and with the customers' needs for quality service.

An increasing awareness of the need for authorities to maximize their human resources has further enabled them to take on and develop equal opportunities policies, demonstrating commitment towards disadvantaged members of society such as minority groups, mature women and the disabled. The emphasis on the value and need for a well-trained and competent workforce has never been stronger, yet the conflicts have equally never been so manifestly and widely obvious.

Authorities are at present having to re-assess training budgets and training requirements for all their employees. Currently, in their revised role as employer, many authorities are taking a more corporate view to training needs across the staffing levels. There is a general recognition that professionals need updating and further training. But that has to be considered in the light of the fact that the vast majority of their employees are not members of any professional body, and may miss out on further training if budgets are tight.

Fears raised by local authorities underline the traditionally held view of public service, only slowly being altered by the changing environment, that employees' training and professional needs should be met totally by the employer.

The professional bodies, however, make it very clear in their literature that Continuing Professional Development is a *partnership* between the employee, employer, provider and professional body.

Role of the professional body

Professional bodies, as previously outlined, take as their prime responsibility the monitoring, guarding and evaluation of quality standards. It is within the bodies' self-interest, therefore, that the membership supports this fundamental attitude. The professions have to work in collaboration with their members; ensuring that they have their willing consent as well as being empowered to enforce the CPD obligation. Here are some comments from those involved in CPD delivery within the professional bodies.

> The IEHO [Institute of Environmental Health Officers] has just completed the first monitoring process of the temporary voluntary scheme (due to be reviewed in '94). The programme was designed to be high access and low cost, with the emphasis away from attending courses. However, there have been complaints from some members [which are being addressed] that by requiring signatures for attendance at conferences and courses, the Institute is enforcing a school-like attitude, as even quite senior managers have found themselves lining up at the end of class to have their documents signed. (Newsum in LGMB, 1993)

The IEHO has recently produced a report based on the results of their first survey of the new CPD scheme, which was carried out for the Institute during November and December 1992. Some of the findings will be of interest to other professional bodies concerned with their members' views on CPD enforcement:

- 51% of respondents had attended a training event during the past month
- very few respondents had paid for their last training event themselves
- 80% of respondents are prepared to attend training events outside working hours
- the average maximum acceptable personal contribution towards a full day course is £35. (Elliott, 1993)

Role of the local authority as employer

For local authorities it is crucial for improvement of delivery and service that the right employees are targeted for training and development. Increasingly, authorities are adopting a corporate strategy towards training needs and requirements, taking an overall view of their employees. The professionals should not account for the major part of the training budget. However, the question does remain: are local authorities committing sufficient of their budget to necessary training?

> Few councillors and officers would disagree with the principle that people are the organisation's most important asset, but is it clearly demonstrated to the workforce?

Commitment is most plainly demonstrated through a willingness to allocate financial resources and time to training
and development activities. Some recent assessments indicate that the average UK training is only 0.14 per cent of the
salary bill which is well below that of other leading industrial nations: 1 per cent in Germany, 1.2 per cent in France
and 2 per cent in the United States. (LGMB, 1991)

What is the employers' responsibility towards CPD provision?

Employers have the right to expect their employees to maintain acceptable levels of professional competence ... whilst
the responsibility for undertaking CPD rests with the individual, the process must be a partnership between employer
and employee. (IEHO, 1991)

In many organisations more money is spent on maintaining
the efficiency of photocopiers than of staff. CPD need not
cost a lot, but it will cost something.

A reasonable staff development outlay for formal training is
1% of annual salary. Many leading companies in the UK
spend up to 3% and in Germany up to 5%. This may seem a
lot, if you currently do not have a specific CPD or staff
development budget.

But even if money is limited, much can be done by adopting
a more positive attitude to professional development and by
using work as a learning experience. The aim should be to
have a systematic CPD programme and budget for all staff.
And don't forget your own CPD needs. (RTPI, 1993)

WHO PAYS FOR CPD?

This question is likely to produce the most conflicting answers as
policies and strategies among local authority employers are still
being created.

Regional employers' organizations offer different points of view:

Internal training officers should be able to put on management courses. For example, that should apply to staff from
any sector such as housing, accountants or engineers.
Courses should be allowed by each of the professional bodies to count for their CPD.

Briefing meetings within the authorities should also be allowed to count towards CPD. We have to begin asking what the cost of all this is to us, compared to our other priorities?

We might appear to be stingy as employers compared to some in the private sector, but then, unlike private employers, not all local authorities yet count in the staff costs of training and development to their budgets.

A regional training officer stated:

We're coming to a rather slow awakening about CPD, largely because it is departmentalized and no one has yet looked at it from a corporate strategic overview. Obviously there is never enough cake to go around and CPD seems to be getting one of the earliest slices, because it is a requirement from the professional bodies – one that is imposed by the outside world.

But maybe we should be taking a totally different approach? Expenditure on training tends to be between 0.5 and 3 per cent of overall pay-roll costs. But should it not be higher in view of growing CPD requirements? Maybe it is time to re-evaluate budgets and create a new budget heading for CPD in its own right? Or should we allocate 1–2 days per employee (not just professionals) for time on CPD?

With growing interest in Investors In People (IIP) we could take the chance to look at CPD as an investment in all staff. Maybe we should not be calling this 'professional development' but simply 'continuing development', to avoid narrowing its focus onto already qualified professionals. That way we would bring in manual workers, technicians and typists.

THE WAY FORWARD?

CPD began for most professional bodies not because of complaints about standards, but because the main work of standard setting on initial entry qualifications had already been developed and settled in a robust way. Now, as highlighted in the LGMB's (1993) publication *Professional Development: Challenge and Change*, the professional bodies have a new set of challenges to meet. Professional development is increasingly being dovetailed into the government sponsored system of National Vocational Qualifications (NVQs) or Scottish Vocational Qualifications (SVQs).

By the end of the century it seems likely that the profession for which there are no competence-based qualifications will be the exception rather than the rule and that the pattern of education and assessment for most professions will be radically altered. (LGMB, 1993).

Fears of competition in the job market

Professional bodies must also keep an eye on competition from other sides of the market. The recession has seen a decrease for many in their memberships, as unemployment has hit the professions. Training and development requirements from the professional bodies should begin to merge with current competence-based thinking, otherwise the increased burden on the employer in terms of resources for extra training could lead to the professional member of staff becoming overpriced compared to a less-qualified technical member of staff from his or her same profession. The local government employer has already begun to consider the requirement for fully professional staff. Often technical grade employees can serve the function as well, and less expensively.

It is therefore seen to be in the general interests of all concerned that local authority employers, professional bodies, the emerging Occupational Standards Councils (OSC), Industry Lead Bodies – and the last member of the consortia: the individual employee – work together in partnership towards the blending of CPD with the higher levels of NVQ (and MCI).

The CPD in Construction Group recently submitted an advisory paper on how they view recent developments. Written by Richard Larcombe, Development Director of the Construction Industry Standing Conference (CISC), this work on recent developments is in its infancy and, as such, is there to stimulate further discussion and development.

There are exciting prospects of using NVQ/SVQ units at the higher levels (Levels 4 and 5) to give a much-needed structure to CPD. Candidates might be required to achieve so many units (or their equivalent) in a given time period to retain their professional status. A log book recording this achievement would be a powerful tool in the candidate's hands and would enhance the reputation of his/her professional Institution. It would also enable employers to recognise and utilise the candidate's potential capability.

Since professional status is generally acquired at the age of 25–30, CPD covers the majority of an individual's total career span. Employers will be reluctant to release staff for long periods for CPD purposes, but the use of open learning techniques would enable candidates to acquire necessary underpinning knowledge towards NVQ/SVQ units (Larcombe, 1993).

NVQs and the lifetime concept of CPD

The natural 'competence decay' of a professional qualification could be avoided by bringing such professional development within the auspices of NVQ Level 5. NVQs are accredited for between three and five years. Part of the Lead Bodies' responsibilities is to monitor legislative and technological changes within their sector. NVQs, therefore, would be seen as the base qualification. The employer and employee would be encouraged to keep up-to-date for further accreditation.

Richard Larcombe comments: 'Two or three NVQ units could easily be the requirement for individual professionals to achieve each year, before renewal of their professional membership was allowed.'

MCI qualifications similarly would be transferable within the NVQ/CPD framework, particularly if MCI modules were contextualized within the requirements of the different professions or different employers' needs. Such a framework would embody an 'operational practice context' with a specific management/policy and strategic overview.

POINTERS FOR FURTHER ACTION

- Professional bodies must continue their excellent work as standard bearers.
- Professional bodies have to bear in mind the changing environment and competitive market. They must work in partnership with employers and ensure that in future CPD provision meets employers' needs and ability to resource, and that it meets the management requirements of the changing work environment.
- Local government employers must assess CPD within their overall training budgets and assessments. They must work together with the professional bodies to achieve the best from the partnerships involved.

- Local government employers also need to encourage their employees to take more responsibility for their own CPD.
- All parties should work with the Lead Bodies towards the development of national standards and NVQ Level 5 so that ultimately CPD can be brought within the accreditation framework.
- Professional bodies and employers have to become more flexible and adaptable to change so that all will survive.

REFERENCES

Elliott, J (1993) *Continuing Professional Development: The results of the survey*, Newnham College, Cambridge (Internal LGMB publication)

IEHO (1991) Consultation Document on Professional Requirements for CPD.

Larcombe, R (1993) Unpublished advisory note.

LGMB (1991) *Achieving Success: A corporate training strategy*, LGMB: Luton.

LGMB (1993) *Professional Development – Challenge and Change*, LGMB: Luton.

LGMB (1994) *Continuing Professional Development – Partnership for Change*

Newsum, D (1993) *Continuing Professional Development: Partnership for Change*, LGMB: Luton.

Stewart, J (1988) *A New Management for Housing Departments*, LGMB: Luton.

Part Two

Individuals

Introduction to Part 2

Part 2 shifts the focus away from the the professional bodies, future trends and particular occupational areas to a consideration of the individuals directly involved and affected by CPD. Contributions identify some of the issues, questions and opportunities which affect the central actors in CPD.

Sandra Tjok-a-Tam's chapter looks at the professional as manager. This role is almost certainly one which was not part of a professional's original education and training but becomes increasingly important as their career develops. Sandra argues that the new Management NVQs (National Vocational Qualifications) can become an essential part of the professional's skill base.

Heather Crockett and John Geale's chapter highlights what they describe as 'the chronic deficiency in the demand for CPD'. Their research at Lancaster University is focused upon questions of the motivation to undertake CPD and uses a group of young professionals to identify what motivates them. The project is at its mid-point and they report some of the interim findings.

Paul Kalinauckas, in Chapter 11, writes about achievement coaching which is a continuous and participative process and is a key part of managers' development of their staff. He describes the coaching cycle, the coaching process and the skills required. He emphasizes that it can be done effectively with all kinds of professionals and managers.

In Chapter 12 Christopher Bond shows another way to enhance and improve the individual's learning. The origins of the portfolio-based approach to professional development are described and followed by the steps needed to construct a portfolio. He ends with some observations on the advantages of this approach to learning, including motivation – a theme also featured in Chapter 9.

In Chapter 13, John Lorriman shows a new approach to Personal Development Plans (PDPs). These have become a popular way of planning future development as well as capturing learning. The software described by John has the potential to make easier and more accessible a process which is often well intended but may be difficult to sustain. He suggests that the 'PDP for Windows' system has numerous advantages for the user over folder-based PDPs.

In Chapter 14 Andrew Gibbons describes his personal approach to CPD. What he describes as a 'low (or no) cost' way of improving competence can be contrasted with the previous chapter's approach to recording CPD. The heart of Andrew's method is his learning logs which he has been keeping since 1987. He describes what he does, what he logs and some of his learning.

The final chapter is by Sandra Clyne. She describes the results of a research project in which she asked a group of professionals about their professional and career development and shows the results in the form of 'professionals' tales'.

9

Improving Business Performance through the Continuous Professional Development of Managers

Sandra Tjok-a-Tam

WHY CONTINUOUS PROFESSIONAL DEVELOPMENT FOR MANAGERS?

The whole process of continuous professional development (CPD) suggests that individual managers take professional responsibility to pursue their own learning and to encourage their colleagues and subordinates in theirs. Yet, in the past, many managers have held a vast amount of practical management experience that has not been fully utilized, by organizations or by individuals, as a means of pursuing their own and their colleagues' learning. Many managers' experiences and cumulative learning had been given little recognition as compared to those managers who hold a professional or nationally recognized management qualification. Often managers attained their job role and status through a professional learning route (Tjok-a-Tam, 1991) that may not have included a continuous developmental process nor accumulated work experience (see Scenario 1). There has been a perceived mismatch between personal and organizational development. Yet it is now becoming recognized that a continuous management development process can form an essential ingredient in the improvement, by individuals and by organizations, of business performance. The linkage between effective performance at work and a manager's continuous professional development could provide a key factor in the survival and future success of organizations in the UK. However this critical connection has not always been recognized.

Scenario 1: Trevor

Trevor was a manager of a specialist service department for a large financial organization. He was in his early 40s and had been at management level for 16 years with the same organization.

Education and Qualifications
Trevor had a professional accountancy qualification – he was not given time or financial support to gain this qualification. He had no managerial qualifications.

Organizational Management Development
He had attended many in-company courses which covered his particular financial specialism plus other management courses such as marketing and people management. He was also given an opportunity to meet people and trainers from other sectors on a three-month management programme which enabled him to '.... develop a less parochial perspective'. The structure, content and delivery of this management programme was of a very high quality. Trevor believed that a management qualification would make little difference to his internal career progress but might enhance his mobility. He felt that within the present economic climate, a lack of management qualifications could have a negative effect on a younger person's desired career progress.

Personal management development
The three-month management programme gave Trevor the opportunity to reflect upon his past achievements and gave him a far broader perspective. Since attending that programme he had given a great deal of thought to his future development and applied for an MBA programme. The MBA, Trevor believes, would develop a 'broader external view of industry and a broader perspective of non-financial areas'. Due to Trevor's extensive experience, especially in the financial sector, a truncated version of the MBA was recommended. However, Trevor's present organization refused to support his application to pursue an MBA, they said, this course 'could provide a mobility passport'. This attitude saddened Trevor, especially as he was a long-standing employee and clearly saw his future career developing within the same organization.

Trevor believed that he needed a work-based learning process that would help him identify his strengths and weaknesses. He also required a process that would help him identify the appropriate top-up training modules for his weak areas. This, he believed, would enhance his management performance. He firmly believed that undertaking a flexible and work-based management programme would encourage managers to go on to further self-development: 'The whole MBA is a daunting task and it would be a waste of time for me to do all the modules, so any thing that would restrict the time would be a bonus'. (Tjok-a-Tam, 1991)

WHY CHANGE THE MANAGEMENT QUALIFICATION SYSTEM?

The Handy (1987) and Constable and McCormick (1987) reports highlighted the generic function of management. Earlier reports (Owen, 1970; Mant, 1969) had also emphasized the need to improve the UK stock of management skills in order to compete with our European neighbours and in the world market. However, in the late 1980s and early 90s a concerted focus was placed on the need for managers to improve their skills and to improve their performance in business. Yet unlike our European counterparts the management function was still not regarded as a 'profession' nor was there any clear-cut way for managers to embark upon a continuous development route. In fact the whole question, 'Is management a profession?' (Deloitte, Haskins and Sells, 1989) was beginning to be addressed by employing organizations, national bodies and educational institutions. This focus on 'management as a profession' was, at the same time, linked to enormous changes in the training and education infrastructure and the entire management qualification system in the UK.

These changes to the management qualification system were brought into effect in the early 1990s and have provided managers in the UK with an opportunity to link their performance and learning at work with a continuous development process and national accreditation. National Vocational Qualifications (NVQs) are one tool that can help managers continuously develop their skills and experience at work *and* improve organizational performance. This provides the key focus for this chapter. The NVQ process is not presented as a panacea for improving business performance but merely as one means of linking work-based performance with a continuous professional development process. Later in the chapter other innovative and individual management processes will be reviewed briefly (ie, the draft

Senior Management Standards and Institute of Directors Standards) together with an organizational review process (ie, the Investors in People Standards).

So how can managers continuously develop their skills and experience through NVQs and at the same time improve business performance?

WHAT ARE NATIONAL VOCATIONAL QUALIFICATIONS?

The National Vocational Qualification system was established in order to improve the stock of skills across occupational sectors and to increase the opportunities for individuals to acquire a higher standard of vocational education in the UK. In 1986 the National Council for Vocational Qualifications (NCVQ), which is responsible for the NVQ system, was established to improve the skills of the whole workforce, from agriculture to warehousing. Other occupational sectors, including counselling and personnel management, are still undergoing a consultation exercise in order for these particular occupational standards to be published in the near future. The government's aim was for 80 per cent of the working population to be included within the NVQ framework at levels 1 to 4 by 1992 and for the remaining 20 per cent of employment, including professional levels, to be developed (DES, 1991). The scope for certificates to be awarded at all levels within the national NVQ framework is increasing weekly (if not daily!)

What is the Management NVQ Framework?

There has been an influx of national Industry Lead Bodies (ILBs) who are responsible for developing and producing the standards of competence for each occupational area. In 1988, the ILB responsible for management standards – the Management Charter Initiative (MCI) – began to lay down the foundation for the framework and approach to the NVQ levels 3, 4 and 5 in management:

- *Supervisory management – NVQ level 3:* describes the general features of a supervisor's role. These features include being responsible for making sure that people work effectively and efficiently, planning and controlling the use of time and materials, helping people to solve problems and managing information. There are seven units of competence which have to be achieved at this level.

- *Junior management – NVQ level 4:* describes the requirements for first line management where the individual is responsible for the direction and control of the activities and work output of other people. This responsibility is a major part of the manager's role. There are nine units of competence which have to be achieved.
- *Middle management – NVQ level 5:* represents the full weight of the requirements of managers operating at a level above first line managers. This level does not however include those directly responsible for the strategic management of their organization. This level may however relate to general managers or individuals managing a specialist function. Level 5 builds upon and incorporates the standards of competence required for first line managers and reflects the broader scope of the role, the need to balance conflicting demands, initiate change and make decisions in more uncertain settings. There are ten units which have to be achieved at this level. (Tjok-a-Tam, in SOLOTEC, 1993)

(Note: when determining the appropriate level to which to work, individual requirements and responsibilities must be taken into consideration. The terms 'supervisor' and 'manager' mean different things in different organizations.)

Management NVQs utilize exactly the same format as non-management NVQs and include functional or task competence statements which are broken down into a framework of units, elements, performance criteria and range indicators. However, unlike other occupational NVQs (except for the customer service NVQ) the management standards incorporate a personal competence model which identifies the personal or interpersonal skills needed to ensure that managers carry out their tasks competently and effectively.

In order to gain an NVQ in management it is necessary to register with an approved centre/provider which will help managers through the process from registration to final award. This whole qualification process can set the groundwork for the continuous professional development of managers.

How Can Managers Use their Experience to Gain a Qualification?

There are many individual managers who have a wealth of experience and knowledge and who also wish to develop and improve their learning and work performance. One of the ways to combine valuable past management experience with a continuous development process is through the achievement of an NVQ in management. This can be accomplished by a manager putting together evidence of performance in a portfolio in order to prove their present competence compared with the management standards which form a particular level of an NVQ. Some managers may find that they already can prove competence against certain units which make up the NVQ, while others may, sometimes with help, identify 'gaps' in their knowledge and experience and find ways and opportunities of 'plugging' them. This process of accrediting proven competent experience is known as the Accreditation of Prior Learning or APL, which is an assessment of an individual's past achievements against, for example, the National Standards of competence or NVQ: 'through a systematic and valid assessment process, an individual's skills and knowledge can be formally recognised and credited, regardless of how, when or why they were obtained' (Simosko, 1991, p. 10).

There are inherent dangers in the APL process which can be overlooked by the manager and by the NVQ provider. Therefore, it is essential that the APL process is perceived by the manager as a method of gaining confidence in what has already been achieved as opposed to what a manager cannot do; and is seen as not just an accreditation device but as an opportunity for learning and a continuous developmental process to improve individual and organizational performance.

The whole NVQ process is not about standing still and gaining accreditation for what can be done now, *it is about going forward* within a continuous development process. This can be achieved either within one NVQ level or by plugging the gaps in experience with new learning opportunities, or by going forward and embarking on another, possibly higher NVQ level.

What are the Benefits of the NVQ Process for Managers?

An NVQ programme can provide a learning mechanism that is both flexible and transferable and which does not necessarily require adherence to a rigid academic calendar or regular attendance at a specific college or external venue (see Scenario 2). NVQ programmes can, by their very nature, supply a work-based opportunity that allows the manager to carry out daily duties and, at the same time, collect evidence from work to prove competence against a specific unit of the management NVQ. It can also provide a continuous developmental tool for those managers who wish to find new opportunities within their organization for learning and improving their performance. However, in order to reap such benefits managers do require assistance and guidance from an NVQ provider who is proficient in enabling the manager to 'reflect-in-action'. Without such 'reflection-in-action' (Schön, 1983) the opportunity for continuous professional development and improvement of work performance may well be lost.

Scenario 2: Chris

Chris's organization is moving from South London to Halifax in three months time and she has collected evidence for four out of the nine units at NVQ level 4 in management. Chris has also collected some evidence for three other units and her adviser has assured Chris that she is on the 'right lines'. Chris is concerned that all the recent hard work in building up the portfolio will be wasted when she moves to Halifax and she wants to know if she can 'transfer' the portfolio to a local centre in Halifax.

As long as the evidence meets the performance criteria contained in the management standards, Chris can 'transfer' the portfolio to another centre in Yorkshire. The whole point about NVQs is that they are based on national standards. All that Chris will need to do is to transfer her registration to another accredited centre in or near Halifax which can then assess and accredit her portfolio. (Tjok-a-Tam, in SOLOTEC, 1993)

What are the Benefits of the NVQ Process for the Organization?

Through a continuous developmental process 'real' work experiences can be used to provide a manager with a portfolio of evidence *and* to develop new opportunities for learning and improvement of work performance. Organizations can discover direct benefits if an action learning approach is integrated as part of the CPD process within a management NVQ programme (Tjok-a-Tam, 1994). An action learning process enables managers to confront and address 'real' work problems within a group or set of managers. Immediate benefits can be seen by individual managers reflecting upon their work experiences and being enabled to supply their own solutions to work problems. Such reflection-in-action (Schön, 1983) assists managers in developing their portfolio of evidence and in discovering new and more effective ways of managing themselves and their team.

An organization, by providing NVQ management programmes in the workplace, can also benefit by saving staff time. The manager does not have to attend an external course but remains in the workplace and integrates her/his own development with key work issues or problems.

This may sound simplistic but in practice it has been found that it is not the content (the standards) nor the framework (the NVQ) nor the willingness of both organizations and individuals to embark upon the NVQ journey that proves difficult – it is the process of continuous development that forms the greatest hurdle.

There are employing organizations which see NVQs in management as a ready-made approach to their management development schemes. There are others who veer away from giving their managers opportunities to gain qualifications that may enhance their 'mobility passport'. There are others who are sceptical of the cost and time it takes for managers to acquire the NVQ through an APL process (Smith and Preston, 1993). All of these views and perceptions may hold some validity in today's stressful working environment. Yet without incorporating a continuous development process within the provision of management NVQs the organization will see neither the positive benefits in improved business performance nor will the individual see an improvement in effective performance as a manager and as a professional.

THE WAY FORWARD

The need to develop the 'profession' of management in order to compete with Europe and world markets has led to a recent focus on strategic management which leads us to a brief review of initiatives in this area. The Management Charter Initiative (MCI) and the Institute of Directors (IoD) have drawn up draft standards for senior managers and for boards of directors. These draft standards reflect good practice at the strategic level of the organization. At the time of writing, both sets of standards are in the process of being piloted with directors and senior managers in organizations throughout the UK.

The MCI Draft Senior Management Standards

The MCI senior management standards combine the framework of other NVQ levels – units, elements, performance criteria and range statements – with a proactive approach to examining the internal and external organizational context. The draft senior management performance standards are grouped into four main areas of action:

- reading and influencing the environment
- setting the strategy and gaining commitment
- planning, implementation and control
- evaluating and improving performance.

Each stands alone and can also interact with the others. The statements describing the underpinning knowledge, understanding and personal competences required are also integrated with each unit, element and performance criteria.

These standards are designed to incorporate the strategic *tasks* required at senior management level as well as the *processes* involved in carrying out the senior management function. The so called 'softer' side of management eg, vision, values and culture of the organization are brought into play within the senior management standards. This combination could provide a powerful thrust for improving the effectiveness of an organization and for providing a process of continuous development for all managers. The piloting of the senior management standards is nearing the end of its phase and it will be interesting to see how and when these standards will be fully implemented in organizations in the UK.

The Institute of Directors Draft Standards

The IoD draft standards aim to provide a framework for boards of directors to review how they are structured, organized, resourced and work. How useful the draft standards are and how relevant they may be to different boards in different circumstances is being investigated during a present consultation exercise: ' ... the acid test of their impact will be the willingness of Boards to examine critically what they do and how they do it' (IoD and Henley Management College, 1994, p. 4).

There is a four-stage framework for the successful completion of tasks and each task is dependent upon how effectively individual directors work together and complement each other. This in turn depends on the personal qualities that each individual brings to bear upon the operation of the board and the personal qualities required for each of the main director roles.

As with the MCI senior management standards, the IoD standards incorporate a range of activities that include, for example, the mission, vision and values that set the broad direction of the organization. Again, it will be interesting to see how the IoD standards are implemented and if any consideration is given to integration with the MCI senior management standards.

These different initiatives illuminate the need for individual managers to retain a clear focus on the process of continuous professional development in order for them to adapt their expertise and skills in today's and tomorrow's dynamic environment.

(A pilot study for SOLOTEC which combines the utilization of the MCI Senior Management Standards with the Investor in People indicators as an Organisational Review tool is being carried out. The third phase of the study is due to be completed in December 1994 and the final evaluation stage will be completed by April 1995.)

The National Standard - Investor in People

The Investor in People standard provides a clear focus for an organizational review and development. It highlights the need and commitment of an organization to develop all its employees in order to achieve the business objectives and may provide an appropriate route for managers to find a mechanism for their continuous professional development. There are 24 assessment indicators, which are divided into four statements or national standards. An Investor in People:

- makes a public commitment from the top to develop all employees to achieve its business objectives
- regularly reviews the training and development needs of all employees
- takes action to train and develop individuals on recruitment and throughout their employment
- evaluates the investment in training and development to assess achievement and improve future effectiveness.

One of the assessment indicators (2.7) refers specifically to NVQs: 'Where appropriate, training targets are linked to achieving external standards, and particularly to National Vocation Qualifications (or Scottish Vocational Qualifications in Scotland)

and units.' Therefore, managers wishing to engage in their own or in their subordinates' continuous professional development could utilize the Investor in People initiative as a means of achieving their aim.

As can be seen, there are numerous initiatives, standards and processes for a manager to pursue in her/his continuous professional development which, at first sight, may appear confusing. I have attempted to describe what is happening now and what may happen in the future, all of which will have some effect upon a manager's continuous development. Some of these national initiatives will, hopefully, be integrated and combined to avoid raising the already high confusion level of so many of today's busy managers. The managers of tomorrow may wish to develop their expertise and skills and by so doing can conform to the MCI mission statement: 'To improve the performance of UK organisations by improving the quality of UK Managers'.

REFERENCES

Confederation of British Industry (1994) *Quality Assessed – the CBI Review of NVQs and SVQs*, London, CBI.

Constable J and McCormick, R (1987) *The Making of British Managers*, London, BIM and CBI.

Deloitte, Haskins and Sells (1989) *Management Challenge for the 1990s – The Current Education, Training and Development Debate*, Sheffield, Training Agency.

Department of Education and Science and Employment Department (1991) *Education and Training for the 21st Century – The challenge to colleges*, London, HMSO.

Handy, CB (1987) *The Making of Managers* London, NEDO and MSC/BIM.

Institute of Directors and Henley Management College (1994) *Draft Standards for Consultation*, London, IoD and Henley Management College.

Management Charter Initiative (1994) *Draft Senior Management Standards* London, MCI.

Mant, A (1969) *The Experienced Manager – a major resource*, London, British Institute of Management.

Owen, T (1970) *Business School Programmes – The Requirement of British Manufacturing Industry*, London, British Institute of Management.

Schön, DA (1983) *The Reflective Practioner. How professionals think in action*, London, Temple Smith.

Simosko, S (1991) *APL. A practical guide for professionals*, London, Kogan Page.

Smith, A and Preston, D (1993) 'APL: The relationship between rhetoric and reality' *Management Education and Development*, 24, 4, 395–405.

Smithers, A (1993) *All Our Futures – Britain's Educational Revolution*, Manchester Centre for Education and Employment Research, University of Manchester (and Channel 4 *Dispatches* programme).

SOLOTEC (1993) *Management NVQs: pre- and post-workshop material.*

Tjok-a-Tam, SA (1991) *The Forgotten Manager*, London, Management Charter Initiative.

Tjok-a-Tam, SA (1994) 'Learning in Action: Developments in management education', PhD Thesis, University of Surrey.

10

The Lone Professional

Heather Crockett and John Geale

Much descriptive work has been done on the *supply* of CPD and on what needs to be done, collectively, to maintain professional competence in Britain. This chapter is based on a current project which starts, and finishes, with the individual. Its starting point was a belief that the critical limiting factor to lifetime learning is a chronic deficiency in the *demand* for CPD. One of the problems with CPD is that a simple process is in danger of becoming over-complicated. The process is essentially simple, but not easy. No one knows this better than the 'lone professional' – a term which many of the project's participants identify as a description of themselves. This chapter will argue that we should all do so.

A short development project entitled 'Stimulating the demand for Continuing Professional Development (CPD) amongst young professionals in NW England' is being funded by the Training, Enterprise and Education Directorate (TEED) at the Employment Department. The Lancaster CPD project assumes that the factors which are most likely to determine the pattern of each individual's CPD concern their motivation, awareness and support, more than the availability of events, materials and courses, important though these are. So the project is investigating motivation and developing generic activities which are supportive. The apparent complications are the result of the differing, and sometimes conflicting, roles of three stakeholders: the employer, the professional body and the individual professional.

> 'I believe I can, to some extent, change the nature of my current post to gain the skills and experience I want.' This stores manager, whose ambitions lie in training, is busy introducing NVQs and studying for IPD qualifications.

Employers, with varying degrees of consciousness, adopt a 'commercial model' (see Figure 10.1) which seeks to develop their

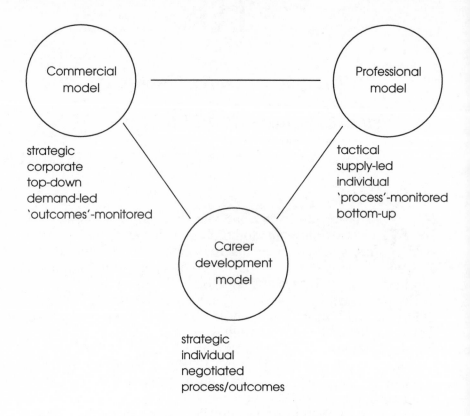

Figure 10.1 *Models of CPD*

human resources to meet anticipated business needs. It is strategic and concerned with the outcomes of personal/professional development, however achieved.

This contrasts with those professional bodies who specify CPD requirements in terms of credits. These, inevitably, are tactical and focus on the process of learning (eg, hours of attendance at formal events) rather than on the skills achieved, or on informal learning.

'If you don't know where you are going, you'll probably end up somewhere else.'

During their initial education and training qualified professionals will have been told what knowledge and skills they require. Others, who have obtained 'professional' status by virtue of their job, are bemused by talk of 'credit' for attending CPD events.

Too prescriptive an education, initial or continuing, can encourage lazy learning, especially if conditioned by too much teaching. This is a major obstacle to CPD, especially when laziness is combined, as it invariably is, with great pressure on time. The CPD process can also be impeded by arrogance and by fear. As the locus of control of a professional's learning moves, when they qualify, from institutions to themselves, much seems to depend on the individual's motivation and confidence to manage their continuing development. Most of our participants felt they were ill-prepared for the new learning skills they have required. But, as they are a self-selected group, they have been motivated to teach themselves.

'I am motivated by new challenges.'

'By taking control of my own development (and not waiting for, or allowing my organization to decide) I hope to avoid becoming alienated, bitter or developing "learned helplessness".' This personnel specialist is concerned with the process of CPD and how to impose structure and discipline which takes account of her own learning style and circumstances.

The principles by which we learn seem to become more complicated as our careers advance, and are likely to make increasing use of informal learning and of other people. Learning goals often evolve.

'CPD is doing deliberately what would otherwise be left to chance.'

They are still purposive and within a general strategy, but come about from knowing how to recognize and exploit opportunities; from managed serendipity. Professional codes should minimize risks, certainly to the client, yet CPD often involves risk-taking.

Traditionally, qualifications are based on formal learning. Even without accreditation for prior experiential learning and the introduction of competence-based qualifications at higher levels, a desire for accreditation is motivating many of the young professionals on the project, both for their value in the market place and to add structure and personal satisfaction; a mechanism for target-setting and for feedback.

'As a lone professional in a large organization, I think it is unrealistic to expect my employer to provide much of what I need.' This occupational psychologist emphasizes his need for up-to-date specialist knowledge. His employability depends on his technical expertise – and his ability to demonstrate this through, amongst other things, accreditation. Also, his job satisfaction comes from knowing his subject.

'I am not interested in trophy hunting.' This police inspector is now aware of what is needed for promotion (which, in his case, is not accredited learning). He recognizes that, 'if I hadn't taken responsibility for my own development, I would still be a PC.'

Some 150 young professionals, all under 40, are participating in the project. It is 'their' project. Just as they must accept ownership of their CPD, they determine the practical development activities which they hope will best provide the encouragement and support they want.

The critical importance of CPD to them all is its link with career development and how it can help them prepare for new opportunities, or to avoid threats (even the threat of being bored). Their primary motivation is neither the business needs of their employer, nor (if they have one) the formal requirements of a professional body; but their own needs.

'No one notices you if you work hard all day. You need to combine work and self-promotion – getting noticed by suggesting new ideas.' 24-year-old woman.

'Say nothing about yourself and you'll stay where you are.' 34-year-old man.

This emphasis on personal ownership, albeit motivated by self-interest, appealed to many employers who have actively encouraged staff to participate. These employees are looking for ways to foster greater individual initiative and responsibility. This approach to personal development (CPD) fits in well with the consequences of flatter organizational structures, more devolved powers and with participative management. These organizations recognize that their staff, as well as themselves, are doing SWOT analyses and developing all-round vision. Individuals are also vulnerable. They are conscious that the world of work, including the professions, is becoming increasingly competitive. As employment becomes more hazardous, the risks involved in professional development may require greater toughness.

Much is said about the cost/danger of not training. Taking one's own CPD seriously is about much more than 'training' and may involve a willingness, by individuals, to take risks. It may involve unfamiliar roles or responsibilities, or using familiar situations in new ways. For instance, staff may decide to use an existing, but somewhat moribund, appraisal scheme as an opportunity for introducing more challenging thoughts on their career and development. This could only apply to members of corporate organizations. A strong motivator for some of the participants is their need to develop support without such an employer. So what sort of things are they doing?

- self-assessment/learning styles
- portfolio building
- career development planning
- learning logs
- mentoring
- networking
- accreditation

These are all topics chosen by small action-learning 'development' groups as one part of the project.

> 'Joining the CPD project has helped me to think about my career, evaluate what I have done and to structure my development opportunities.' This senior staff nurse has responsibilities which span nursing, management and education. Like many professionals, her career could move in a variety of directions.

We like the initials 'CPD' because the permutations of 'C' and 'P' around the 'D' for development are illuminating. The link with career development planning has already been mentioned. There are also professional development portfolios and personal development plans. The different terms, maybe, give another insight into some unnecessary confusion. The activity we are concerned with is lifelong and individual, it is continuous personal development. It should apply to everyone and, where support is coming from employers, they may well wish to avoid 'professional' elitism in their own HRD policies. It is also often difficult, if not impossible, to distinguish between 'personal' and 'professional' competences.

As professional careers develop, *individual* practitioners have quite different learning needs. These can become confused with the needs of professional *groups*. Professional bodies must, within the context of their collective CPD:

- research, evaluate and implement changes in professional practice
- identify, train (and accredit) educators to manage change in their profession
- respond to society's changing demands
- redefine the skills, competences and knowledge required by new entrants to the profession
- encourage CPD.

'Each year I report my formal CPD to my professional institutions, but I do much more than the requirement.' This senior planning officer has set himself both long and short-term goals.

'The initiative must now come from me.' This recently 'chartered' engineer has received excellent company training for his short-term technical requirements. His need is for a longer-term plan and for complementary management skills.

These are very different requirements from the process of self-assessment, personal goal-setting and self-directed learning being undertaken by the project's 'young professionals'. We have said earlier how many felt let down by their initial education which inadequately prepared them for this. The project, therefore, plans to develop, with one pre-registration student group, activities which will better prepare them to take charge of their own CPD.

The lone professional may need to learn from a number of different professions, learning to use different professional concepts, or even languages. They become professional 'magpies'. The research scientist may need to develop marketing or financial expertise. Whereas professional bodies may need to define professional boundaries, some practitioners will move outside their own professional 'tribe' and become enriched by other 'cultures', while retaining their basic identity.

The project, in mid-1994, is half-way to completion. It has surveyed some 150 participants and identified the practical activities, such as portfolio preparation, listed above. Each is being developed by small, self-programming groups meeting across the region who are able to use consultants as and when they wish. It is about taking responsibility and learning that, even if we are lone professionals, there are ways we can promote our own development.

Some participants are, literally, 'lone professionals' without the support of an employing organization or even a professional body. Many others are single professionals providing specialist expertise within an organization as, say, a statistician, microbiologist, personnel officer or plant engineer. CPD is not, however, necessarily private. A recent study from Hull University (Gear *et al.*, 1994) has shown how important people are to the whole process. Some of the obstacles to CPD (lack of time, isolation, competition, arrogance, timidity, laziness, etc.) have already been mentioned. Another is lack of awareness of what CPD is and how it relies on other people:

> As long as professionals think of continuing learning in terms of external inputs, resources and requirements, they will tend to ignore their main resource, which is one another (Gear *et al*, 1994).

Lone professionals should be less susceptible to the dependency/complacency syndrome, but how do they tap into support from others? Some have easy access to 'networks' and can establish informal 'mentoring', should they wish; others have to work much harder to find relationships which work for them. This project has provided one such an opportunity. Other young professionals are known to have enrolled on courses as much for the 'networking' opportunities as for the curriculum. Indeed, some organizers of part-time and open learning courses have recognized this and build in appropriate mechanisms.

Our evaluation of the project at this half-way point has identified at least five different ways in which participants are benefiting from it:

- it has helped them to take the initiative for, and therefore control of, their own development
- this helps, in turn, to improve their relationship with their employer, avoiding disappointment and fostering mutual respect
- it has offered membership of 'networks' which are non-threatening and which lead to:
- self-knowledge and 'getting it straight in my mind'
- a more structured and disciplined approach to longer-term personal development.

'Belonging to a CPD group has made all the difference; it has built up my confidence and helped me to focus on where I want to be.' This management graduate has had a number of career changes, blaming successive employers for her frustration.

For many the problem is how to balance conflicting demands. Professionals, and those on the project are typical in this respect, are establishing learning habits and the pattern for their CPD in the earlier years of their careers when the financial, family and social pressures on them are greatest. Perhaps we can get some insight into how they achieve 'balance' by looking at their answers to what constitutes successful CPD. Primarily it must, of course, help them to do their jobs; it must be judged on performance criteria. These criteria involve changed (professional) behaviour. But 'successful CPD' seems also to be associated with relationships: with other 'lone' professionals, with employers and, possibly, with those who help us to keep our balance. Change also involves growth.

It will be interesting to see what emphasis is placed, by the young professionals themselves, on any ways the project has helped them to develop feelings about themselves, their values and their self-esteem.

'Structuring my CPD has, to my amazement, greatly increased my job satisfaction!'

REFERENCE

Gear, J, McIntosh, A and Squires G (1994) *Informal Learning in the Professions*, Hull University.

11

Coaching for CPD

Paul Kalinauckas

INTRODUCTION

Coaching is increasingly being recognized as an essential element in any successful CPD process. Effective coaching of the individual committed to continuous professional development will open doors to realizing more potential. However, coaching is an underutilized skill and frequently missing from many CPD initiatives. Without ensuring that good coaching is integrated into CPD plans they are likely to fall short of achieving their potential. At worst, CPD will become another short-term initiative or mechanical, mandatory series of tasks to be carried out to meet the requirements of organizations or the professional institutions.

One guide to good practice in CPD (The Engineering Council, 1991) refers to coaching as a process in which a manager, through discussion and guided activity, helps a member of staff solve a problem or carry out a task better. The focus is on practical improvement of performance and development of specific skills. This rather task-based approach to coaching is called 'management coaching'. However, individuals intent on raising personal performance recognize that professional development and personal development are inexorably linked. In order to develop professional skills and expertise you also need to develop and grow as a person. After all isn't that what lifelong learning is really all about?

For individuals committed to their own lifelong learning a more sophisticated approach to coaching is required. Kalinauckas and King (1994) coined the phrase 'achievement coaching' which is defined as a continuous and participative process whereby the coach provides both the opportunity and encouragement for an individual to address his or her needs effectively in the context of personal and organizational objectives. The difference here is that the focus is primarily on what the individual wants and how this fits with the requirements of the organization rather than the other way around. Professional people are generally smart enough to realize that organizational demands temper personal ambitions and they do not head off in pursuit of purely personal achievement without benefit to the organization. In order to coach effectively within the context of CPD you have to start with the individual's agenda. Working from what the organization alone needs is not conducive to gaining commitment to ongoing CPD.

Futurists John Naisbitt and Patricia Aburdene (1993) predicted the shift towards the individual's agenda. The move from a controlling approach of management towards a leadership approach, that they recognized, demanded the development of coaching capability: 'To lead you must learn to coach, inspire and gain other people's commitment.' They predicted that the new workforce of the 1990s would help organizations achieve their objectives only if they could achieve their own personal objectives as part of the bargain. All this may seem a bit idealistic and a far cry from the more familiar approach of sacrificing personal desires for professional success. However, the price that some professionals are required to pay in terms of bowing to organizational dictate is nowadays not so willingly exacted.

Without this ability to achieve personal objectives the individual's focus will inevitably drift towards scanning job advertisements or considering early retirement! National press reports have identified a possible trend of professionals being less prepared to sacrifice themselves solely for the benefit of the organization. Often the realization that there is a yawning gap between what they want and what they actually have only surfaces after several years scrambling up the career ladder. Throughout their careers they hear about the things that they can and can not do. Guidance is usually only given on a skills level; rarely are they asked what they really want to do.

WHAT IS ACHIEVEMENT COACHING?

At its simplest, coaching is about bringing out the best in people. Achievement coaching is about finding out what they really want and dovetailing this with organizational objectives. It is the

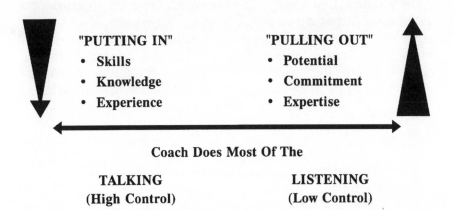

"PUTTING IN"
- Skills
- Knowledge
- Experience

"PULLING OUT"
- Potential
- Commitment
- Expertise

Coach Does Most Of The

TALKING
(High Control)

LISTENING
(Low Control)

Figure 11.1 *The coaching spectrum*

developmental end of the coaching spectrum that really appeals to the professional embarked on the path of CPD, more than the controlling approach to skills development. The spectrum of coaching ranges from the coach literally 'putting in' skills, knowledge and experience to the person being coached, to the 'pulling out' of potential, commitment and expertise (see Figure 11.1).

This requires considerable versatility on behalf of the coach to identify at which end of the coaching spectrum they should be operating. The only way to find out is to work from the other person's agenda. The coach does this by using 'listening questions'. By asking questions about personal objectives and ambitions and listening intently to what is being said, the coach is able to guide the professional along their personal path of CPD. This is more than just another form of career counselling. It has to explore personal vision, values and beliefs and how these are linked to organizational vision, values and beliefs. That way a genuine commitment to action is gained. It is only by putting effort and action into the process of CPD based on both agenda that the individual *and* organization will benefit. A win-win scenario is what is needed for CPD to really flourish.

The key skills of coaching are listening and questioning, deliberately put in that order. Listening involves other interpersonal skills such as paying attention to the other person, showing that you are listening by nodding and smiling, building rapport and mirroring body language, A full list of the skills demonstrated by competent coaches appears below. To be an effective coach these skills need to be developed – all part of the coach's own CPD!

active listening
questioning skills
giving praise/recognition
building rapport
creating trust
being non-judgemental
being candid and challenging
being able to work from the other's agenda
giving encouragement and support
focusing on future opportunities
getting to the point
observation skills
being objective rather than subjective.

These skills can be developed through practice and a few simple exercises are included in this chapter to help the budding coach.

Cynicism, scepticism, distrust and fear are some of the obstacles to be overcome in putting effective coaching for CPD into practice. The lack of coaching skills inherent in most organizations was identified in a research report on their use as a managerial tool (Huthwaite Research Group, 1990). This is probably why management guru Charles Handy (1989) stated that learning needs to be facilitated not by a boss or supervisor but by a neutral coach from inside, or often from outside the organization. A report into the recruitment, retention and training of new graduates in the UK (Graham and McKenzie, 1994) noted coaching frequently mentioned as an integrated part of the graduate development process in company recruitment brochures. However, the research came across very few instances where coaching actually took place.

The achievement coaching process is one used by professional coaches working with senior executives in industry and commerce. It focuses on identifying and clarifying personal vision and then gaining commitment to the actions necessary to achieve it. Inevitably it leads to a process of self-coaching being established to avoid dependency on the coach. The achievement approach to coaching has been successfully applied in both the public and private sector. Professionals in specialisms as varied as accountancy, engineering, law, marketing, personnel and sales have all benefited from achievement coaching. The management development manager of a major building society commented, 'My introduction to achievement coaching convinced me that this is a powerful management method for building on the untapped potential of individuals.'

THE COACHING PROCESS

Achievement coaching as a process is carried out in an environment of trust and honesty. The role of the coach is to encourage the individual to articulate and commit to action whatever needs to happen in order to achieve personal objectives. It has to start in the current reality perceived by the individual but is focused on future opportunities. It asks the questions, 'What has to happen for you to get what you want?' and 'How can you achieve your personal as well as professional objectives?'

Personal vision, lifetime goals, objectives and the balance of life can be explored during an achievement coaching session. This must be carried out using an objective and non-judgemental approach. The concept of discussing a personal vision may be new to some individuals and at first may be treated with some scepticism. Once the initial barriers are overcome the results, both for the individual and the organization, pour out. Possible obstacles or barriers are discussed together with options to overcome them. Achievement coaching is based on the premise that ultimately the individual knows what is best for them and has all the internal resources to achieve what they want. They may not yet have accessed all their internal resources or inner power; the coach has a role to play in helping them discover those for themselves as well as identifying and overcoming self-imitations.

You do not have to be an occupational psychologist to coach others effectively. Although most coaching processes are intrinsically simple they are not necessarily easy to apply. One of the biggest barriers to coaching that the coach needs to overcome is the fear of not knowing as much about a particular subject as the person being coached. They are still stuck down the 'management coaching' end of the spectrum based on enhancing skills and solving problems for people. The developmental end of the coaching spectrum necessitates the coach adopting a less controlling approach. By listening and asking questions, the person being coached will eventually come up with their own answers to what needs to be done. The coach can make suggestions but must break out of a 'command and control' approach to achieve success. Where technical or skills input is required, the coach moves down the 'putting in' side of the spectrum with the permission of the individual being coached. Approaching skills input from the developmental end of the coaching spectrum is very powerful indeed.

Creating a future scenario is a very strong approach. To avoid it becoming an idealistic dream it also needs to take account of possible obstacles. Successful coaching is firmly based on moving towards future opportunities rather than exploring past problems. That is what distinguishes it from a counselling based approach. The model in Figure 11.2 demonstrates the key difference between coaching and counselling. Coaching take place primarily in the top right hand corner whereas counselling starts in the bottom left corner; they overlap somewhere in the middle.

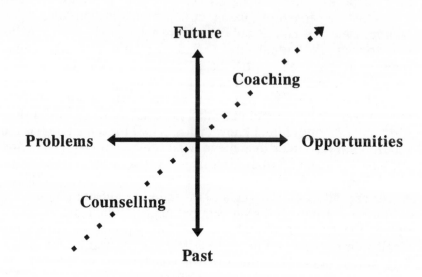

Figure 11.2 *The difference between coaching and counselling*

A simple exercise to help towards establishing personal vision is to go through the following process; it can be done alone or with a coach. The exercise entails thinking through or discussing future opportunities: what do you see yourself doing, achieving or being in the future? This can be based solely on professional objectives or widened to include personal ones. Choose whatever timescale you like, one year, five, ten or more depending on your personal timeframe. Write a statement on how you see yourself in the future and then complete the rest of the form.

PERSONAL VISION

I see myself

....

....

So that I can

....

....

Possible obstacles

....

....

Actions (what and by when)

....

....

This format can be used again and again for creating positive statements about the future, linked to realistic action plans. It is particularly useful in the process of CPD as a way of checking if you are on track. The pursuit of technical knowledge and qualifications alone can become a fruitless exercise if it is not linked to personal vision. As one professional commented, 'I have committed a lot of time and resource to my CPD. I am well qualified and abreast of the current requirements of my profession. However, although I enjoy the acquisition of further knowledge I don't have a sense of purpose as to how this is helping me get what I want out of life.'

THE COACHING CYCLE

The coaching process is directly linked to action. One of the tests of effective coaching is whether or not the person being coached does anything towards their CPD. A hard-nosed, operationally-focused senior manager in a large organization suddenly realized what it was all about when discussing the effectiveness of coaching: 'Now I know that what I thought as meaningless conversations that you were having with people was effective coaching taking place. They always seemed to lead to the other person becoming energized and getting into action.' The coaching cycle is an effective way of accelerating ideas into action. The cycle illustrated in Figure 11.3 starts with the conceptual aspect of decision making and leads through to implementation, completion and review – a simple process but often as not missing in practice.

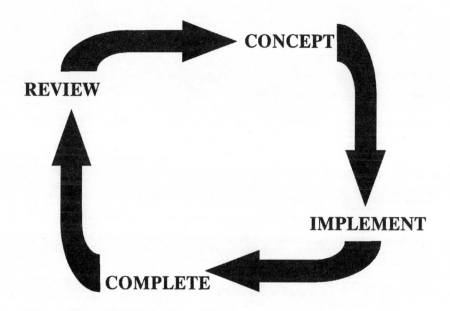

Figure 11.3 *The coaching cycle*

The Coaching Cycle falls into four stages; as described below.

Concept

All goals and projects start with an idea which either appears one day in our mind or is suggested by someone else. We then go through some form of creative process to work the idea through before making a commitment and a decision about the resources we will need, the level of priority and our commitment to action. Many goals or projects remain at this stage and fail to be implemented for all sorts of reasons. The coaching cycle allows you to explore the reasons for lack of implementation. Here, the coach is concerned with what the person does to avoid implementation. What kind of avoidance rituals do they fall into to avoid getting what they want? Is it a short five minute ritual like going for a cup of coffee, a chat or telephoning someone, or is it a longer avoidance ritual like just hoping it will go away or continually putting it to the bottom of the pile? If these rituals can be identified then the person being coached has a choice: they can either continue with the ritual and realize that they are doing so, or they can get back on the cycle to achieve their goals.

Implement

This is all about getting down to action. Ideas that seemed good ideas at the time may become less attractive once they require action. Sounds familiar? Some people are good at getting on with the early stages of implementation and get bored soon after. Others find it difficult to complete and get stuck at 95 per cent completion, sometimes not finishing things off to avoid being judged or wanting to achieve perfection. Again they may engage in avoidance rituals preventing completion.

A common technique which assists in implementation is to break the project down into small manageable tasks and focus attention on these rather than the overwhelming size of the whole project. One way of doing this is to get the person being coached to think through the small steps and decide what they are committing themselves to to get a 10 out of 10 by the end of the week or month ahead. For example, is it realistic to start learning another language as part of their CPD this week or to find out what options there are to learn the language, such as buying a book, some tapes or finding a tutor?

Complete

Completion is crossing the t's and dotting the i's – what needs to happen to get finished and move on. Were clear outcomes set at the start so that one would know when they have been achieved, or have the goalposts moved? Once the initial outcomes are achieved, do they get stuck into the next project immediately or make time to review? Most people have lots of different projects going on at the same time and are trying to achieve several goals. However, to increase energy and maximize personal productivity they need to complete the final step of the coaching cycle.

Review

Completing the cycle involves a combination of acknowledging success, reviewing what went well or not so well, giving and receiving feedback and celebrating successful completion. The purpose of completing the cycle in this way is to put more energy into the cycle. It is not uncommon to feel tired and lacking in energy at the completion of a project. Just imagine having completed a long report that you have sweated blood to complete within the deadline; it is unlikely that you will feel immediately energized to get on with the next one. There is a period of time required to recharge the batteries and raise motivation. Using the definition of motivation as 'having a motive for action', completing the final stage of the cycle acts as a reminder of the motive by reviewing the stages of the project or goal and remembering the original concept. It also acknowledges our success in completion.

Reviewing tasks and projects is an underutilized skill. The pace of the modern world encourages us to move on to the next task in haste and does not allow precious time to be wasted going over old ground. However, a vital part of learning is the review process without which valuable lessons can be lost and mistakes repeated. It is particularly useful to review not just what was done but also how it was done. A common coaching point is, 'If you had to do it again, how would you do it differently?'

Celebration adds the icing to the cake by rewarding successful completion. In coaching you may occasionally ask what has been set as a celebration once you have completed – what reward are you going to give yourself? Because we are motivated by pursuit of pleasure, having a celebration in mind can help when the going gets tough during implementation. It could be a simple matter of having a celebratory drink after work, a meal or buying some new clothes. This all helps to reinforce a sense of wellbeing and satisfaction and is not to be underestimated.

Internalizing the coaching cycle as a way of getting ideas into action supports the process of CPD. The negative effects of frustration, loss of confidence and self-esteem, tiredness and feeling out of control that result from continually stepping off the cycle can be overcome. Keeping to one's commitments and continually reprioritizing while staying on the cycle is a fine balance to be achieved. However, the payoffs that accrue of more energy, greater motivation, self-esteem and confidence, as well as recognition, lead to higher levels of achievement, which is what CPD is surely all about.

CONCLUSION

These coaching exercises will help those intent on developing their skills as coaches. Becoming an effective coach is a lifelong learning process and immensely satisfying. Developing coaching capability in organizations is an essential part of CPD. Without it any attempt to encourage professionals to commit to CPD may end up with only tokenism, notches on the qualifications ladder or half-filled but underutilized personal development planners. A survey (Huthwaite Researched Effectiveness, 1990) of over 350 organizations in the UK and the rest of Europe identified coaching as by far the most popular development method predicted to grow in application over the next 20 years. Now is the time to sharpen up on coaching skills and concentrate on developing coaching capability within organizations. Professionals committed to CPD will welcome the support of a coaching-based approach to maximize the benefits to themselves as well as their organizations.

REFERENCES

The Engineering Council (1991) *Continuing Professional Development – the practical guide to good practice*, The Engineering Council, London.

Graham, C and McKenzie, A (1994) *Delivering the Promise – Recruiting, training and retaining new graduates*, Yellowbrick Training and Development Ltd, Glasgow.

Hammer, M and Champy, J (1993) *Re-engineering the Corporation*, Nicholas Brearley, London.

Handy C (1989) *The Age of Unreason*, Business Books, London.

Huthwaite Research Group (1990) *Coaching Skills and their Use as a Managerial Tool*, Huthwaite, Rotherham, England.

Huthwaite Research Report (1990) *20:20 Vision Survey Report*, Huthwaite, Rotherham, England.

Kalinauckas, P and King, H (1994) *Coaching – Realising the Potential*, IPD, London.

Naisbitt, J and Aburdene, P (1993) *Megatrends 2000*, Futura Publications, London.

Webster, S (1994) *The professionals who prefer MeJobs*, Independent on Sunday, 7 Aug.

12

A Portfolio-based Approach to Professional Development

Christopher Bond

INTRODUCTION

It is now generally acknowledged that education and training are a continuing and lifelong process. It is also increasingly clear that education may take many forms, not all of them traditional. No longer can a person's education be associated exclusively with the period of induction and learning which occurs in the first 20-odd years of life. Nowhere is this more evident than in the professions.

The pace of scientific, technological, social and political change is now so rapid and intense that an initial period of professional or occupational training can only provide the foundations of knowledge, skills and attitudes on which further development must be built, if it is to remain current. When we consider how quickly knowledge can pass its sell-by date we start to appreciate the importance of lifelong learning.

The feeling amongst many involved in education, training and development is that a greater emphasis must be placed on learning rather than teaching or training. If we are to compete in a global market place and be on the 'cutting edge' then a knowledge of how to learn is as important as the content of what we learn. There is, therefore, an increasing emphasis on teaching people how to learn as well as teaching specific content or skills. Portfolio-based approaches to learning can enable individuals both to learn new content or skills and to gain valuable insights into how they learn and so enable them to be more effective learners.

WHERE HAS THE CONCEPT OF PORTFOLIOS COME FROM?

Portfolios are not an entirely new concept. Indeed my colleagues at the University of Central England in the Faculties of Art and Design and the Built Environment frequently remind me that this is 'old hat' to them. Portfolios as collections of material created by an artist probably go back several hundred years. In order to win commissions from patrons, artists would produce designs, plans and sketches of previous work as evidence of competence. What is new is the application of the concepts of a portfolio-based approach to learning and development by a number of more traditional subject and professional disciplines.

The recent explosion of competence- and outcome-based approaches to education, training and development has seen an enormous marketplace evolve for portfolios. Many learners have sought to construct portfolios in their attempts to gain certification for their prior knowledge and skills. Here I wish to look not at portfolios in the context of accrediting prior learning but rather at how a broader based view of portfolios can be used as a means of structuring and recording continued professional development.

PORTFOLIOS AND THE HRD PRACTITIONER

Many of us would argue that we are always learning; after all, in the human resources field our whole focus is on development. While I would not question that basic assumption it is true to say that when asked to articulate or reflect on what we have learnt, trainers are not always able to do so as clearly as we should.

Honey and Mumford (1989) have identified four basic approaches. A portfolio-based approach would be particularly relevant to the retrospective and prospective approaches that they identify. The retrospective approach identifies and produces a record of past achievements and is essentially looking back at what has *been* done. In contrast, the prospective approach engages the learner in a process of planning to learn, taking and making learning opportunities and reviewing and applying the learning gained from such an approach. The concept of a professional development portfolio offers an excellent mechanism by which to capture such a dynamic and iterative learning process.

The preparation of a portfolio is in itself a useful exercise in self-evaluation, organization and integration. The process of portfolio building is as important as production of the completed product. Portfolios require individuals to exhibit critical self-reflection on current skills and knowledge levels, identify areas for further development and plan ways in which new learning can be acquired. In this sense portfolios offer individuals a unique opportunity to direct and monitor their own learning and development. Portfolios then are about a process of education and development largely controlled by the individual learner.

Portfolios require individuals to relate their learning to clearly set and measurable outcomes, to exhibit critical self-analysis and to demonstrate an ability to present information in a clear and concise fashion. These outcomes may be predetermined in the form of existing national standards or professional body requirements. In the context of CPD they may be standards set by the individual learner and negotiated with a mentor or members of a peer group action learning or development set.

Portfolio-based approaches to learning and development offer a mechanism by which the individual can truly direct and monitor their own learning and development. Portfolios can be used as an excellent self-development tool and there are a variety of uses to which the finished product can be put. Some of the possible uses to which a professional development portfolio may be put are:

- as evidence of competence to practise
- to demonstrate readiness for promotion
- for job interviews/assessment centres
- to increase self-confidence/self-esteem
- for a personal competence/skills audit
- to gain academic recognition/credit via credit accumulation or the accreditation of prior learning
- as a basis for staff appraisal or peer review
- as a resource bank for case study material
- as an educational/developmental exercise
- as a means of changing job role or function
- to record development over a specified period of time
- as a tool for critically evaluating one's own practice
- a source of relevant information for new entrants to the profession/organization.

WHAT IS A PORTFOLIO?

Portfolios are personal, particularly in the context of their use for CPD, and will often reflect the character and personality of the individual involved in the process. For this reason I hesitate to offer a model format for a portfolio. Part of the benefit of portfolio-based approaches to learning and assessment is that the individual learner is allowed room for creativity and exploration.

Given the diverse backgrounds and areas of activity in which HR professionals operate it is unlikely that one model of portfolios will evolve. Indeed in a dynamic and evolving profession room needs to be left for creativity, imagination and individual application of the process of portfolio construction. My own view is that, armed with a number of general principles of good practice, individuals should be allowed the scope and freedom to develop their portfolio as best suits their requirements. The more reflective individuals in the profession may find use in reflective diaries and critical incident analysis while others might prefer a more active approach by including such items as video or audio cassettes of their practice.

Figure 12.1 gives an outline of some items that might be included in a professional development portfolio. It is illustrative in nature and by no means gives an exhaustive list or set of prescriptions.

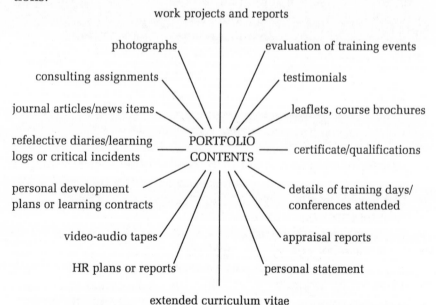

Figure 12.1 *Contents of a professional development portfolio*

Professional development portfolios are designed to assist in identifying training needs, to help us to make and take learning and development opportunities, to record and monitor these experiences and to provide evidence for self-assessment or by peers on our competence to practise. They offer an exciting and challenging method of structuring our own personal development plans.

The process of constructing a portfolio is a learner-centred educational experience. It requires the portfolio constructor to relate their learning to predetermined learning goals, to structure and record learning from experience and to demonstrate their ability to present their knowledge and skills in a clear and concise fashion.

In this sense an important consideration in constructing a portfolio is being clear about your motives for doing so and who the intended audience might be. These two factors will have a significant effect on the purpose, nature and structure of the portfolio. For example, a portfolio designed for a job interview will need to be clear, concise and concentrate on your practical skills, competences and achievements to date. On the other hand a portfolio as part of a self-negotiated development programme for which you are seeking academic recognition will need to demonstrate your ability to reflect on and in practice, to conceptualize, to apply theory to practice and at higher levels to develop personal professional theories of your own.

PORTFOLIO CONSTRUCTION

A professional development portfolio is designed to give an overview of your personal experience and to demonstrate significant areas of learning and professional competence derived from both formal and informal learning opportunities. It involves you in a process of self-evaluation, needs determination, reflection and action planning. In seeking to prepare a professional development portfolio for CPD purposes you should bear in mind the following points of good practice:

- its structure should be accessible and clear to both yourself and any potential assessor or reviewer;
- it should include a clear contents page to enable speedy recovery of relevant material;
- it should be professional in style and appearance;
- it should include a personal statement at or near the beginning which sets the portfolio in context and gives the reader

an overview of its purpose and the character and personality of its owner;

- it should make clear reference to any national or personal standards/learning objectives against which the portfolio has been constructed;
- it should include items which evidence your professional competence and learning that has occurred in the course of your professional practice;
- all items included in the portfolio should be clearly referenced and indexed with a summary sheet indicating their place and purpose in the portfolio;
- evidence included in the portfolio should demonstrate what you have learnt from experience or other sources and how this learning has impacted upon the way in which you discharge your professional duties;
- if your portfolio is to be of real value then it will not assume the status of a finished product in that it will be continually updated, reviewed and added to as your circumstances change.

Where Do I Start?

Preparing a portfolio takes time and will not happen overnight. It is a developmental process which requires thought, planning and action. The starting point for a professional development portfolio will be the drawing up and agreeing of a personal development plan or learning contract. There is, however, an important stage before the plan is drawn up, which is to establish what your current skills and abilities are. This can be achieved by undertaking a personal competence audit identifying your current knowledge and skills base.

Having located our starting point we are ready to work on our personal development plan. This acts as our personal route map along our journey of personal development and portfolio construction. The stages in this process can be likened to setting out on a simple car journey and are identified below.

Stage one: the first stage is to determine where our starting point is. In order to achieve this we use external points of reference and conduct a personal competence audit. This is not dissimilar to my consulting a map, looking around me for external signs and confirming my location prior to starting a journey.

Stage two: having determined our starting point it is good to think about where our journey might be leading to. Rarely do I get in my car without some conception of where I might be going. I do not necessarily have to have a firm destination in mind but some general idea of whether I am heading North, South, East or West is useful. The same is true of learning, particularly in an experiential context. As we are directing and initiating our own development it is important that we set ourselves some clear learning goals. These help to focus our attention on learning from our experiences and help us to make or take relevant learning opportunities. I have found that discussing my proposed learning goals with a peer or mentor has helped me to refine my key learning objectives and to set myself realistic, attainable and challenging learning goals for my personal development.

Stage three: the next stage involves my considering what route I might take to reach my destination. When I embark on my car journey I have a clear route in mind. Deviations from my plan sometimes occur as I come across roadworks or a stationary queue of traffic. Such deviations, however, do not throw me off course as I still have a clear idea of my ultimate destination and make contingency plans as appropriate. Similarly in learning we can plan what type of development activities we need to be involved in to assist us in achieving our stated learning goals. We can exercise a degree of personal preference over what type of learning activities best meet our needs and plan our journey accordingly. Also we can exercise choice over the pace of our development and choose whether we head off on the fast track motorway route or take a more leisurely pace on the A roads.

Stage four: finally, before starting our journey we need to check that we have access to the resources we will need. In the same way as I check my oil and water, stock up on boiled sweets, drinks and choose my favourite driving cassettes, I need to think about what resources I will need to assist me on my learning journey. What books or journals will I need access to? Are there any short courses or conferences that could assist me on my development path? Do I need to negotiate to try out some new duties at work? Such planning is essential and continually helps us to focus on meeting our declared development needs. Colleagues, managers and friends can be invaluable in assisting us with the resources we need for our personal development. It may, for example, be possible to use your personal development plan and portfolio as the basis of future appraisal interviews.

Stage five: I now start my journey of personal development using my personal development plan and portfolio as my guide. At this stage I can start collecting evidence to put in my portfolio which demonstrates progress towards meeting my learning objectives. In the same way as I might buy postcards or take photographs on my journey, I collect reports, certificates, video excerpts of a training session I ran, etc. and start to place them in my portfolio. Rather than continually struggling with my filing system to find appropriate evidence I now include items in my portfolio as a matter of course. Of course the evidence I collect should be relevant to my learning objectives. A postcard of Snowdonia seems entirely inappropriate if my journey took me to Devon!

Stage six: the final stage in the process is to review and evaluate one's self-development and the journey taken when you have reached your destination. This can act as a celebration of having achieved a number of learning goals and increase motivation to reappraise our new skills and knowledge base and plan for further development. Continuing professional development is ongoing as its name suggests, so having achieved our goals is not the end of the journey but only the start. Who knows, maybe next time, with my recently acquired skills and knowledge, I may take a plane or boat rather than use my car!

SUMMARY

One of the most significant findings from research about self-directed learning is that when individuals go about learning something naturally, rather than being taught or trained, they are highly motivated and usually learn more rapidly (Boud, 1985; Rogers, 1983). In my experience of working with a diverse range of client groups on portfolios I find that individuals tend to be more motivated towards learning, learn more deeply and permanently and with greater enjoyment when they are placed in control of managing and directing their own learning.

In the context of CPD it is often more appropriate to allow learners greater freedom in determining and monitoring their own development needs. Portfolio-based approaches provide a vehicle for making learning a negotiated process between the individual and their mentor or peers. In summary, some of the key advantages of a portfolio-based approach to learning are that:

- it encourages you to take responsibility for managing and

directing your own continuing professional development;

- it offers a process by which you can record and monitor your own professional development;
- it helps you identify what you have learned from your experiences so that you may become a more 'reflective practitioner';
- it helps you collect and collate evidence for formal reviews and appraisals;
- it assists you in meeting the requirements of any professional bodies' policies on CPD;
- it can assist you in the process of claiming credit or recognition for your continued development;
- it increases self-confidence, motivation and the capacity to learn;
- it ensures that the learning you acquire is relevant to meeting your needs, those of your organization and your profession;
- because you enjoy it!

REFERENCES

Boud, D (1985) *Reflection: Turning experience into learning*, Kogan Page, London.

Honey, P and Mumford, A (1989) *The Manual of Learning Opportunities*, Peter Honey, Maidenhead.

Rogers, C (1983) *Freedom to Learn*, Merrill, New York.

13

Using Software for Personal Development Plans

John Lorriman

WHAT ARE PERSONAL DEVELOPMENT PLANS?

How much of our real potential do we really release in ourselves? Is it 20 per cent, as Professor Charles Handy suggested in a recent talk at the Institute of Directors? Or could it be very much higher?

In order to get the best out of ourselves, we need to learn as effectively as possible. This implies very strongly that we need to structure and capture our learning and target our career development. Some form of document to do all this for us is essential; without such documentation the vast majority of our daily learning is quickly forgotten and we tend to drift in our careers, concentrating on dealing with short-term problems, instead of sitting back and thinking through a structured career strategy. The usual term given to such personal planning documents is a Personal Development Plan (PDP) and they can take many forms, including folders and software. The approach which I will describe in this chapter shows how software is used for PDPs.

THE CONTEXT IN WHICH PDPs SHOULD BE USED

My experience shows that PDPs are only effective if they are used in the right context. There are three essential components, shown in Figure 12.1, which I call Lorriman's windows. This figure shows the importance firstly, of individuals having a missionary approach to their self-development. They must use PDPs, take responsibility with missionary zeal for their own competence and career development, and not be reliant on others for their CPD.

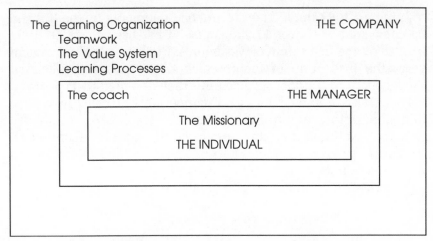

Figure 13.1 *Lorriman's windows*

Second, it is essential that their manager acts as a coach, a subject Paul Kalinauckas covers in more detail in Chapter 11. As far as I am concerned, *the most important role and skill of a manager is the coaching of staff*. The ability to coach should be a major part of their initial training as managers and it should be the prime basis on which they are appraised and promoted.

This brings us to the third factor: the company as a learning organization. This requires a value system which is consistent in recognizing and rewarding individuals who use PDPs and managers who act effectively as coaches. There must also be as many opportunities for learning created as possible and this requires teamwork throughout the organization.

I have introduced PDPs into many organizations and soon learnt that they are only effective where *all three* of these windows are in place. These can be described as windows of opportunity, and where any one of them is missing the organization will miss many opportunities to maximize its learning.

I have been closely involved with PDPs since I first read about the idea in The Engineering Council's (1986) discussion document, *A Call to Action*. At the time I was a member of the Institution of Electrical Engineers' (IEE) career development committee and suggested that one of their ideas – that of using 'personal record log books' – was one we should develop in the IEE.

We designed a document we called the Professional Development Record (PDR), which was piloted with 200 volunteers in GEC Telecommunications, where I was controller of training. In 1987 the PDR was launched nationally by the IEE and has now sold well over 11,000 copies. It has been adopted under licence by the Institution of Mechanical Engineers, and for several years the Institution of Incorporated Electronics and Electrical Engineers used it under licence until they designed their own.

I was also involved in The Engineering Council's own PDP pilot, and helped to introduce PDPs into organizations as diverse as Abbey National, London Underground and AEA Technology. In most of these cases the PDPs were based on loose-leaf folders which were both simple and attractive to use, though I started to use a software approach in one organization.

WHY USE SOFTWARE?

We should be continuously looking for better ways of doing things. In the case of PDPs, I am convinced that enormous opportunities are being opened up to us by the knowledge revolution. Microsoft Windows, for example, has made software very much easier to use – and very importantly much more fun, while hardware is tumbling in price. The explosive growth of the Internet in the 1990s and of groupware, in particular Lotus Notes, makes it increasingly important for us all to use software to learn from each other.

Folder-type PDPs are fine in many ways, but they are very much like individual atolls in the Pacific; beautiful as they look from the air, you do wonder about the difficulty in getting from one to another! In addition, we are likely to see more and more virtual organizations, where relatively few people are employed directly by an organization, and instead the experts are hired as and when needed. The ability to look quickly at someone's experience, set of competences, area of expertise and so on, makes some sort of PDP software very attractive. All this suggests that PDPs which use software have clear advantages over traditional approaches. The particular form of software I am describing has been developed from the work with The Engineering Council and the IEE outlined earlier in this Chapter.

THE DATAEASE PDP FOR WINDOWS

In 1993 I worked with DataEase, who have the largest share of databases in the UK and are very active elsewhere in the world.

I helped them introduce a CPD system, centred on a PDP based on their own software. This new concept, which we have called 'PDPs for Windows', was launched in 1994, together with my colleague Ron Young, through Knowledge Associates Limited, the software company specializing in knowledge management.

The type of screen we use to make it simple and attractive for users is shown in Figure 13.2. The user sees a screen which closely emulates a folder-type PDP, and which is personalized with their name.

If we open the off-the-job training page of the PDP, we can enter details in the screen shown in Figure 13.3. In addition to a description of what you have done, you can add details of the benefits and the proposed follow-up actions. More importantly, this learning experience can be directly tagged to a key competence, a sub-competence and an element, and if necessary to more than one of each of these. In the box at the bottom right of the screen, the user can also identify whether this is a technical/personal/short-term/long-term learning experience.

There is also a similar screen in the software to record and tag day-to-day learning experiences. In many ways, this is even more important than off-the-job training, since it is where most of our learning comes from. Unfortunately most of us do not record or structure this learning and 'PDPs for Windows' is likely to play an important role in revolutionizing the way in which we go about recording and structuring our CPD. If something is important, *measure it and monitor it*, then apply feedback to improve things.

Using Reports to Improve CPD

A large number of reports have been designed into our software, which can be tailored to the requirements of each customer. Figure 13.4 shows the wide range of reports which are available. Figure 13.5 shows one of these – the reports on the off-the-job training – which demonstrates how the software allows us to monitor the dates on which key competences, sub-competences and elements had learning experiences tagged against them. In addition, it shows the number of hours of each experience, the total for each employee and the total for the organization as a whole. Under 'Search reports', these statistics can be interrogated within specific dates. Furthermore, the software shows the balance in learning experiences between technical/personal/ short-term/long-term for each employee. 'PDP for Windows' software also enables you to:

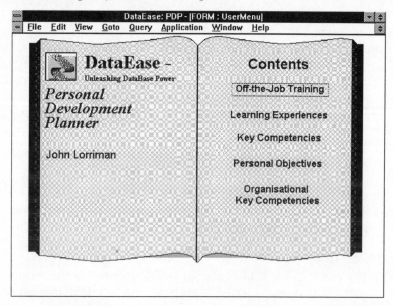

Figure 13.2 *Opening screen for PDP for Windows Software*

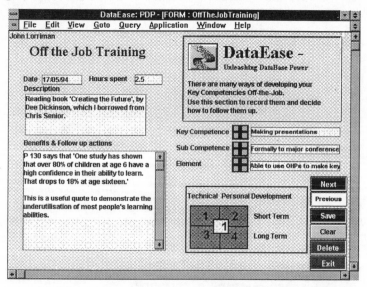

Figure 13.3 *Typical entries for off-the-job training*

- allocate levels to key competences, sub-competences and elements;
- enter a date by which these must be reviewed;
- provide the initials of the person who has authorized the levels of competences and review dates;

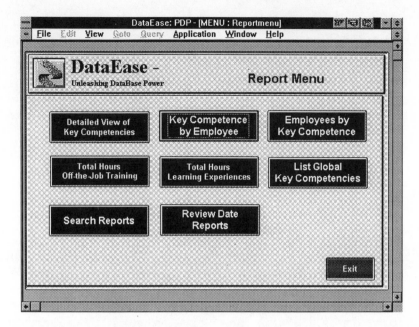

Figure 13.4 *Report menu*

DataEase: PDP - [REPORT : QOTJTOTALS]					

23/08/94   **Total Hours Off The Job Training**

John   Lorriman

Key Competence	Sub Competence	Element	Hours	Date	Area
Facilitating	Small groups of up to 6 peopl	Read body language	3.3	05/08/94	3
Making presentations	Formally to large groups		2.3	07/08/94	2
Facilitating	Medium sized groups up to 1		3.3	07/08/94	3
Facilitating	Small groups of up to 6 peopl	Listening skills	3.4	09/08/94	2
			12.3		

Ron   Young

Key Competence	Sub Competence	Element	Hours	Date	Area
Writing skills	Writing leaflets and flyers fo	Able to structure the materi	3.3	03/08/94	4
Writing skills	Writing handouts for Courses	Able to structure the materi	22.0	08/08/94	2
			25.3		

Jill   Lorriman

Key Competence	Sub Competence	Element	Hours	Date	Area
Able to design PDPs	Able to design folder-type PD	Able to liaise with clients to i	44.5	02/08/94	1
Able to use software pa			22.9	04/08/94	2
Able to design PDPs	Able to design software PDPs		33.9	02/08/94	4
			101.3		

Figure 13.5 *Report screen*

- monitor automatic flags which come up to indicate when any key competence, sub-competence or element is either within 30 days of the review date or when the review date has expired.

The way in which the user sees this information is shown in Figure 13.6. A # appears if the review date of a key competence is within 30 days of expiry and ## if the review date has already passed; these two aspects – imminent and expired review dates – can then be monitored in the reports part of the software.

Making Appraisals Work

The integration of appraisals and CPD is a critical aspect of a professional's development and the employee's involvement in the process. It is unfortunately relatively rare to find an organization in which appraisals work effectively. The only way in which appraisals can be successful is if they are a stock-check on the ongoing CPD of an individual. People can only reach their targets if they are continually developing their competences in a structured way and if this competence growth is linked directly to their appraisal targets. This requires both commitment by each individual to their ongoing competence development and sup-

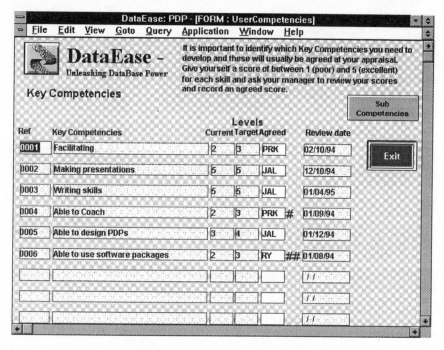

Figure 13.6 *Key competences*

port from their manager acting as a coach. (These and many other issues critical to the success of CPD are discussed in detail in Lorriman *et al.*, 1995.) There are many facilities available in this software, including the ability to enter details of the objectives derived from the appraisals, for each individual.

One other very important feature we have designed into 'PDPs for Windows' is the option for any individual to look at the key competences required of any other job in the organization. Anyone can then see what the gap is between their current set of key competences and those required for the post they are aiming for – and thereby their CPD can be focused on their real needs, both long- and short-term.

PDPs FOR LOTUS NOTES

Lotus Notes is by far the most successful groupware anywhere in the world. Some organizations have tens of thousands of their staff, as well as their clients, linked together with this software.

In simple terms, Lotus Notes breaks down the barriers of space and time. It is possible, and frequently happens, that learning is so fast in a worldwide organization that someone finds that a colleague in Australia has had a problem, someone in Europe has found a solution and colleagues in the USA have been able to use this solution to a problem they never knew existed – all before the colleague in Australia has started work!

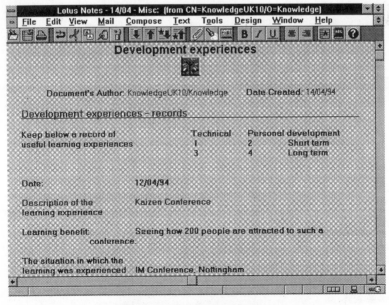

Figure 13.7 *Lotus Notes*

Ron Young and I have developed a range of PDPs in Lotus Notes. One example of a screen from this is shown in Figure 13.7.

SUMMARY

PDP software can put energy into a CPD system to an extent which it is almost impossible to do in any other way.

Almost everyone involved in CPD agrees that PDPs give structure, form and discipline to the process. To add to the traditional 'folder' approach a new method which uses the latest in IT means that there is more flexibility, responsiveness, accessibility and the possibility of sharing your data with your coach/manager. Given that you have a portable PC and a modem you can use the PDP programme any time, anywhere in the world to engage actively in your CPD. One final question then remains. Since all the evidence is that the Japanese are not as comfortable with software as Europeans and Americans, can this PDP software at last give Europe and America the edge in learning over Japan?

REFERENCES

The Engineering Council (1986) *A Call to Action – Continuing education and training for engineers and technicians*, The Engineering Council, London.

Lorriman, JA, Kalinauckas, P and Young, R (1995) *Upside Down Management – The only way to win*, McGraw-Hill, Maidenhead.

14

A Personal Approach to CPD

Andrew Gibbons

BY WAY OF INTRODUCTION

This chapter begins with a short introduction then gets straight into the methods I have used to work on my own CPD over the past eight years or so. Emphasis will be placed on low (or no) cost ways of improving competence. Although what I have done seems to work for me, I'm not suggesting that these are the *best* or universally relevant ways to go about it. The purpose of this chapter is to give you, the reader, a glimpse of my rather eccentric, some say obsessive, efforts to keep getting better at what I do.

I take CPD more seriously than most, and that's right and proper; after all, as a 'trainer' (which is what others call me; personally I'm comfortable saying I help people to learn, but more about that later), it's a good idea to be seen to practise what I preach.

SO WHAT DO I DO?

Since February 1987 I have kept a learning log of everyday developmental experiences. A blank example is shown in Figure 14.1. This is the main way I record my CPD (although at the time I didn't know it would be called this). In the seven and a half years between my first and most recent entry I have written 795 entries, averaging around two a week.

Let me briefly lead you on a tour of the learning log so you'll see how it works. Firstly the 'significant experience'. This is a one-line description of the event or incident that prompted me to get writing. I tend to write this last, to reflect what was written. One of the things I've learned about tracking and recording my CPD in this way is that it is hard to project the actual developmental

THE LEARNING LOG	DATE:	NUMBER:
Significant Experience		
What happened?		
Conclusions		
Actions		
When?		

Figure 14.1 *A learning log*

value of what is perceived at the time as a 'significant experience'. Something I felt at the time would be amazingly developmental, and logged accordingly, might turn out to be worthless in learning terms, just as an event that I felt at the time had no developmental value may, perhaps some time off and as a result of unforeseeable circumstances, prove to have been significantly developmental. It's a bit hit and miss, but by consciously looking for the really significant experiences I'm *more* likely to find and make good use of them than if it was left to chance.

'What happened' is for a brief outline of the event or experience itself. By brief, I mean no more than 70 or so words. If I'm not careful I get carried away, moving into 'conclusions' which, for me, is the crucial section, as it pushes me into actually reflecting on what happened, which I find really tough. If I've kept the 'what happened' bit tight, there may well be scope to pinch space for some additional lines of conclusions – significantly, all of which start with 'that', an excellent concluding word.

Once I've noted typically between 10 and 20 conclusions, I move onto 'actions'. It's been hard enough up to now, but this is the really painful bit, as these prod me into committing myself to what I will do as a result of the conclusions.

This is of course crucial, as otherwise the time and effort taken in writing up the significant experience and concluding is not as likely to lead to actions which indicate true learning. The 'when' section may be time-oriented, for instance 'by the end of the month' or 'during the week ahead', or they might be situational, for example 'next time I meet these people' or 'when I next have a chance to use these skills'. The key with committing to actions is to keep them to a manageable number (which I find means between three and six) and avoiding vague statements like 'soon' and 'whenever I can'.

Entries normally take no more than 25 minutes to complete, and average around 400 words. This may sound like a big commitment, but most us can find an hour or so to dedicate to our CPD.

SO WHAT DO I LOG?

A lot of people feel their jobs don't offer much in the way of development opportunities. From my experiences I feel that every job, and to broaden this a little, every life is full of them, and that the problem is more likely to be that we tend not to recognize them, or fail to see the potential for applying the learning from one experience to other, often unrelated contexts. It may help to briefly give an insight into just four subjects that I have written about many times since I commenced logging in February 1987.

Interpersonal Issues

For a lot of us, professional competence will be dependent in no small way on how well we get on with people, and the development of interpersonal skills. My learning log is full of reflections and planned actions that focus on my own and/or others' behaviour. This means that observations of listening, tolerance, empathy, the working of meetings, team and group behaviour, and individual interactions figure prominently. Interactive behaviour provides a limitless reservoir of potential learning experiences, and I have written many entries on issues such as listening, body language, in/sensitivity, interruptions, praise, and criticism.

Time and Stress Management

Lots of scope to learn and develop here. Although I see value in formal, structured course-based training, there's nothing more powerful than reflecting on my own behaviour, planning how to make better use of my time, and lessen stressful incidents. Attending a time management course may result in things being done differently and better, but too seldom is this the case. Reading an article on time management may be thought-provoking, and hit home with harsh realities, but what will change as a result? Writing learning log sheets that focus precisely on *my* in/actions, and plan how *I* can use time more effectively for me at least mean a time- and cost-effective, needs-based alternative to costly, less directly relevant methods of developing competence.

Customer Care

Is there anybody who in the past month has not had an irritating experience as a customer? Strange isn't it that in spite of the millions spent on customer care training we still see so little *real*, sincere concern shown to those who buy products and services. If we are to learn – meaning do something long-term as a result of these experiences – then writing them up in a learning log entry can be a worthwhile investment.

Noting briefly what happened, consciously recording conclusions in terms of feelings, observations, and effects, then planning definite, time-based actions to *implement* that learning can result in more development than an eight-foot pile of well-written articles or a lifetime of training events. The difference is that it's all about your experiences and how you will be able to use them as learning events and thus to develop.

Managerial In/Competence

I have learned an awful lot from the hundreds of managers with whom I have spent time over the years, and it may well be that I've learned more from those who are not models of ideal practice. This is an important principle for anyone who wants to make the most of everyday developmental opportunities – we don't need *positive* experiences or experiences; there's a lot to be learned from imperfection.

The four sample subjects above indicate I hope, how most, possibly *all*, experiences provide scope for the opportunistic and motivated self-developer. The basic idea is to turn the largely accidental process of development into a deliberate and planned process by, for instance, making the most of informal, everyday experiences from which we can learn.

Just for good measure, some of the other things I've logged over the years include the following:

Induction	Organizational issues	Change management
Quality	Recruitment and selection	Consultancy
Appraisal	Motivation	Marketing
Selling	Domestic issues	CPD
Counselling	Writing skills	Successes and failures

WHAT KEEPING A LEARNING LOG HAS HELPED ME TO LEARN ABOUT CPD

Here is a very short summary of some of the things I've learned about recording CPD in a learning log.

As a very personal approach to managing my own learning, keeping a learning log has helped me to understand that too little training results in learning, and that training is but a small part of *development*. By this I mean that a lot of us manage to develop ourselves without coming within a mile of a training course, and that too few training courses result in sufficient long-term application of learning to make their cost in time and money worthwhile. The central issue is *learning*, which I define as a long-term change in behaviour resulting from an experience. Training without learning is all too common, and is not worth a lot – if anything at all. Development, on the other hand, implies learning, and does not depend upon training.

Learning is a unique, personal and voluntary process, and any formal, course-based method of developing people by training should, but all too often does not, recognize this. I am concerned that too many who should know this appear not to do so. We *all* have development needs, no matter how experienced and competent. In fast-moving professional environments all competence has a 'sell-by date' so past expertise can become obsolete if not topped up by new learning. In addition, we all have *limits* to our development; it is not possible to be as good as the best in all we do no matter how hard we try. An accurate assessment of the parameters of competence and its determinants can be a worthwhile (and developmental) exercise.

There are other variables at an individual learner level that significantly influence the likelihood of any potentially developmental event or experience resulting in long-term learning. One such variable that has enjoyed prominence over the years is learning styles. This means that we learn in different ways, and that some of us have a preference for *doing* things, becoming easily bored, seeking and valuing activity over reflection, which in turn often results in short concentration spans and little long-term learning even from those events and experiences that were fun, exciting, or whatever. The thought of keeping a learning log would not appeal to many of these people – and as one myself, I found the structure and discipline it demands really hard work, but it has helped me to learn by becoming more reflective. On the other hand, more naturally reflective people may think to the point of procrastination, finding the thought of taking responsibility for managing their own development daunting, and prefer an unhealthy dependence on others to 'train' them.

A learning log can provide material, hard copy 'evidence' of learning and development, in a format that can be adapted to suit individual needs and issues. This may for instance mean that naturally reflective people reduce the space for, if using my layout, 'what happened' and 'conclusions', as they will gain more by confronting the pain of an extended 'actions' and 'when' section that prompts the *use* of learning that may otherwise be merely fine words.

The motivation to learn has, regrettably, received far less attention than styles. This is a pity, as the implication of the style research may be that by matching style with the right type of learning opportunity, development will occur automatically. This is not the case often enough, and I feel it is because we must be motivated in order to learn, and that those whose motivation is strong will overcome barriers others will find insurmountable. The barriers may be an 'incompatible' learning style – for instance too much reflection for the liking of those who want to do things all the time. Other barriers might be a workload that gets in the way of developing professional competence; domestic responsibilities; or boss and colleague disinterest. The strongly motivated learner will take their CPD sufficiently seriously that these or other barriers will not stop them getting better at what they are paid to do.

The insights that keeping a learning log to record CPD has given me have brought home the fact that learning itself is a skilled process, and that the ability to direct our own development demands the use of specific and valuable competences that have applications way beyond the developmental. From my experiences I suggest that the most important learning skill is the ability to seek and accept advice and feedback. There is a big difference between seeking advice and feedback and *taking* the advice that results. Some people are good enough at asking for advice, then 'yes but' when they get what they sought.

Skilled learners never reject advice and feedback out of hand, and don't feel threatened by approaching people for their perspective on an issue. Even when they don't hear what they want, they are sufficiently interpersonally competent to avoid instant dismissal of what they receive in response to the approach. People normally like having their views or advice sought, and I have learned a lot (thus developing professionally as a result) from becoming adventurous, for instance 'phoning or writing to people whose views – often in print – interest me.

Feedback can be hard to invite and take, and too few people give this with sensitivity and in the constructive way we all want. That said, for as long as we rely upon self-assessment of our competence, we may be losing out on the views of others who may, if honest and accurate in their evaluation, be more help to us than years of insularity.

THERE'S A LOT IN THREE WORDS

Continuing Professional Development has three significant strands:

Continuing – meaning just that, and suggesting an unbroken process

Professional – differentiating between *personal* and professional issues, and

Development – distinguishing itself from training; CPT would mean something very different.

So, CPD should be continuing, and that's most easily achieved by truly integrating working and living with learning and developing. For me this means not seeing my development as being something I do in addition to other aspects of my life – both domestic and work – but as an important element of both. In this way I never have to set aside *any* time to work on my CPD, as I am constantly seeking to identify and make the best use of developmental experiences that everyday life puts before me. As a more skilled learner than I used to be, I'm better at spotting and exploiting potentially developmental incidents and events than I was, but I still have a long way to go.

The 'P' in CPD is worth reflecting upon, as *personal* and professional development may be two very different things. For me the two are very often hard to separate, and some professional work, as mine, involves such a breadth of activities that a case can be made that all personal development has professional relevance. I feel some professional bodies are too rigid in their definition of professional activity, leaving insufficient flexibility to reward those whose developmental activities are clearly more personal than professionally oriented. A highly motivated self-developer should not have a big problem making a case for personal development to even the most structured of professional bodies, so long as s/he can indicate convincing, if indirect, linkage between apparently unrelated experiences. Only the more 'grown up' professional bodies recognize and value such development which, particularly when informal (ie, not course-based) is harder to administer and quantify than what is called 'input'-oriented, easily measurable events.

So to the 'D' word, and to many other issues. My self-directed efforts have led me to believe that I learn far more from everyday experiences than training courses. Well, that's hardly a startling revelation, but I'm saddened by the prominence formal, structured, often but not always course-based activities have within so many CPD schemes. It is administratively convenient for professional bodies to pretend we learn more from training than development in the wider sense, and this suggests that those who value hours or days of measured inputs instead of accepting the unquantifiable nature of true learning and development should be running CPT schemes, as clearly training is preferred to development. Many of us get a lot better at what we do without coming within a mile of a training course.

MY OTHER CPD ACTIVITIES

Returning specifically to my own approach to CPD, in addition to my learning log, I do some other things, described below.

Television and Radio Programmes

As I'm typing this, the video downstairs is recording an Open University programme on 'leadership'. It may well prove to be of no value to me and, if so, after watching it in the next day or two I will record over it. On the other hand, I may add it to my library of currently 123 programmes on 29 tapes, which represent a wonderful reference resource. My video library, which was started less than two years ago, has been a real help to review and note a programme in advance of an event, or 'just' to broaden my knowledge on topics of interest.

Reading

I'm sure there are very few professional people who don't read journal articles and/or books on topics relevant to their particular specialisms. That said, how much do we actually remember from all those hours of reading, and how well organized and accessible are the articles? Without question, I have learned plenty from my reading, but then I go about it in a far more structured and deliberate way than I used to. For instance, to take a recent example, a book of 223 pages yielded 9 pages of well-spaced notes, probably not much over a thousand words of quotes, lists and key points. I find this is well worth the effort. After all, why invest hours of precious time reading a book when, especially after a few weeks have gone by, little or nothing can be recalled or used? By producing a permanent record of what has been read, I have a resource that means the reading time was not wasted, and that the reading results in my doing things as a result – after all, knowing isn't learning, and development (CPD) is all about putting new knowledge into practice.

Networking

Over the years I have developed and maintained a growing network of people who are significant sources of development. It takes time and effort to keep the network operational, and books full of telephone numbers of people you've had no contact with for months do *not* constitute a network! One test of the effectiveness of networking is ringing someone you've not spoken to for a while, and finding they've moved on since your last contact. For me, networking means seeking and sharing information of interest, and I have many developmental items and sources that have resulted directly from my network. An inherent issue of networking that is more than periodic telephone chats is that of unequal benefits. It is inevitable that one person will gain more than the other in any developmental network, as precisely even splits are not possible. The way through this I have found is to view any networking relationship as long term, and to recognize that balanced reciprocation is never possible. Actively networking has given me access to my network partner's networks, which significantly broadens my perspectives and development.

A Learning Group

For the past three years I have been a member of a learning group, which consists of a half dozen people who meet every three months or so to discuss matters of concern and mutual interest, and often to work intensively on specific issues. For those of us without direct colleagues, or who do not enjoy close and developmental relations with those we have, a learning group can be a way out of the isolation of lone working. I find contacts between meetings of as much value as the meetings themselves.

Training Courses

Yes, I do use these to bolster my CPD activities, although very selectively: after all I'm self-employed, and paying for my own development tends to make me particularly concerned that courses meet my real needs, and that I will do enough, long-term, as a result to justify the cost and time off. My self-directed efforts can go so far, but there is a role for genuinely developmental courses and seminars to supplement my other methods, and enable me to benefit from others with skills and knowledge I will never possess.

IN CONCLUSION

Those professionals who show genuine interest in their own development will welcome the opportunity CPD provides to recognize and reward efforts made to constantly update and improve. Inevitably, there will be plenty who resist this, playing the 'I didn't get where I am today by showing interest in my own development' card. For those of us who enjoy the support of professional bodies that legitimize everyday learning instead of imposing formal, training-based activities that fail to recognize the individual nature of learning and development, CPD should present no major problems. After all, it's *your* development, and what you learn belongs to you and no one else. When all is said and done our CPD is a portable resource.

Finally, the word 'development' implies and suggests change, and for the better. This in turn means that the skilled learner, who makes a success of CPD, will be constantly striving to move beyond the bounds of current competency, inevitably taking risks, innovating and, in all likelihood, making mistakes as the comfort of the well known is left behind. For CPD to be a success we need to move away from blame cultures, and value more those who confront and challenge the status quo, seeking new ways and trying new ideas. This happens too rarely, but remember, it is possible to be the only one who's right!

FURTHER READING

Here's a selection of articles I recommend you read if you want to learn more on the issues raised above.

Artingstall, B (1982) 'Learning through self development', *Journal of European Industrial Training*, 6, 1.

Farnsworth, T (1979) 'How to develop yourself', *Management Today*, May.

Gibbons, A (1994) 'CPD – whose learning is it anyway?', *Training and Development*, March.

Greene, M and Gibbons, A (1991) 'Learning logs for self development', *Training and Development*, February.

Hinton, I (1984) 'Learning to manage and managing to learn', *Industrial and Commercial Training*, May/June.

Mumford, A (1981) 'What did you learn today?', *Personnel Management*, August.

Mumford, A (1990) 'The individual and learning opportunities', *Industrial and Commercial Training*, 22, 1.

Pearn, M and Downs, S (1989) 'Developing skilled learners', *Industrial and Commercial Training*, May/June.

Pedler, M (1985) 'Self development – with a little help from your friends', *Training Officer*, July.

Ray, L (1984) 'Management self development', *Training and Development*, October.

Salaman, G and Butler, J (1990) 'Why managers won't learn', *Management Education and Development*, 21, 3.

15

Individual Professional Development Stories

Sandra Clyne

INTRODUCTION

These personal accounts of professional development have been included in order to:

- provide a glimpse of the individuals who are affected by the issues and questions which are addressed in this volume
- show the diverse, complex and inventive ways in which people develop their careers and maintain their professionalism
- examine some of the ways in which careers and professional development happen
- identify some of the qualities and behaviour shown by professionals in their continuing professional development at different stages of their career
- see if there are any identifiable patterns in their approach to their professional development.

This investigation was set up as a small research project to look at the overall question: *How do professionals manage their professional and career development?*

The method chosen was to select a small sample of professionals and carry out semi-structured interviews. The sample was chosen to cover various criteria, including:

- both women and men
- traditional, 'older' professions
- newer, '20th century' professions
- an age range from 20s to 50s.

The professionals selected were either personal contacts or professionals found for me by others.

The interviews used as the main question: 'Tell me about your professional development starting with your first study period or first job'. This was supplemented by further questions to ensure that I captured both initial qualifications and CPD in response to the requirements of a professional body, employer or a change in career direction. I took notes, transcribed them into 'The Tale', sent this back to the interviewee for approval and/or correction and produced a final draft.

I decided to ask questions about initial qualifications as well as CPD in order to take an holistic view of the CPD process as part of lifelong development and learning. Although CPD can be defined as the formal schemes which professional bodies have for their members, much of this book confirms a much broader view of CPD.

There is no suggestion that the transcribed interviews constitute a definitive picture of how professionals manage their professional development. Instead, it is in the form of a snapshot which shows some of the ways this particular group have managed their career development and their differing forms of CPD.

Although the focus of the book is CPD, this only plays a small (albeit vital) part in these stories. Before you get to formal CPD you have to become a professional. For some this is a straight route from university to professional qualification and then maintenance of this through formal CPD. For others, the route may take many twists and turns. Increasingly, because of the changes in society described by a number of contributors to this book, people may find that they need be more than one kind of professional during their working life.

Because professional development is a process and not a destination, we are seeing CPD as lifelong learning and learning for life. It cannot be left entirely to chance and must be managed in a way which is congruent with a person's career, professional development and the changing circumstances of their life.

THE ARCHITECT'S TALE

Training/Education/Qualifications

I am a Chartered Architect having achieved the qualification through five years full time study followed by two years professional practice.

Thinking about my CPD, I suppose it has always been part of

my professional experience. Even in the early days of training I was required to keep a logbook which used a framework provided by the Royal Institute of British Architects (RIBA) to ensure that during the initial period of professional practice I had some experience of most aspects of the services expected of an architect. This logbook formed the basis of regular reviews and discussions with my supervisor.

CPD in my Professional Life

I worked in private practice for ten years and in a local authority for a further ten. During this time, my professional practice has involved CPD. It is driven by the projects I carry out. As it is impossible, and unnecessary, to know about and keep up-to-date with every aspect of architectural practice, my CPD is on a 'need to know' basis. I decide, on behalf of my clients, what research needs to be done. Whatever I'm designing I consult the profession's journals, RIBA's library, the practice's own guidance documents and my network of contacts for advice and help.

There was little or no difference in my approach to CPD in private practice and local authority work. In each, there is a need to keep up-to-date because of constant changes in building regulations and developments in architectural and building practice. Acquisition of knowledge is driven by a need to do the best job I can for the client.

Projects are often organized under the direction of a senior partner and developed in detail by a team of professional architects. Because of this way of working, there is a community of peers and we take the most relevant experience of each and apply it to the project. If there are new elements which no one can cover, we identify who will take responsibility for researching this and bringing knowledge and guidance back to the team. In this way we learn from each other.

New Requirements

Since the early 1980s there have been changes in the profession's code of conduct, new pressures and opportunities. These mainly stem from the changes which have identified the 'marketplace' and 'business planning' as key elements in business success. Since the time of Wren, architecture has had a strong artistic element which is now generally described as 'design'. Most architects spend the bulk of their time at the drawing board designing buildings and the details of their construction and setting. Of course, there has always been an element of business awareness to keep practices solvent, but this has primarily been the responsibility of the senior partners. Now it is has become everyone's responsibility and this requires the development of business appreciation and new skills.

In addition, architecture has traditionally been a 'gentleman's' occupation with business conducted through word of mouth and by reputation. Architects have not been allowed to advertise and potential clients had to consult the RIBA's Practice Register. This has now changed and architects can advertise and promote their practice. This means that there are new skills to be learnt in the areas of customer care and marketing.

Riba's CPD Scheme

The Institute has been slow in adopting a formal system of CPD partly because of the traditional view that '... architects do CPD every day of their lives ...' However, there is now a scheme which describes CPD as:

> ... the activity which maintains, enhances, or increases the knowledge and skills of the member to the benefit of his or her capabilities as an architect [and] CPD is an individual responsibility designed to ensure sound professional development (RIBA CPD policy document)

The annual CPD target is 35 hours and the preparation of a Personal Development Plan is recommended. Methods of assessing your needs, of achieving your targets and recording activity are also shown in the scheme. It is seen as each architect's duty to do CPD but RIBA does not intend to monitor compliance.

My Current Position

I am no longer in general architectural practice and for ten years or so have worked in the technical and education department of a trade association. This means that I am able to extend my professional experience into new areas. These include writing and lecturing, teaching undergraduates and construction professionals and monitoring the latest developments in a very technical field. I have to liaise with other trade associations, technical committees, industry and working groups. I also continue to develop new competences in my own time – recently I attended a public speaking course and am working at becoming more computer literate.

All in all, CPD, in whichever form it takes, plays a significant part in my personal and professional life. I understand the need for formal systems and believe that structured programmes can be a great help in focusing effort, but to really work, it has to live within you.

THE COMMERCIAL AIRLINE PILOT'S TALE

Background

I began my working life as an engineer for a ferry company. This really set the pattern for my later move to aircraft – a combination of travel, a highly complex technological environmentment, responsibility for the smooth working of a complex machine plus responsibility for the lives of the passengers. However, the complexity of the maintenance of a ferry was as nothing compared to the technological sophistication of a modern passenger aircraft.

The Move to Aircraft

The initial academic requirements for the post of trainee pilot were two 'A' levels and five 'O' levels but the selection process was long and rigorous. It involved days of interviews and tests. Out of 20 interviewees only two were accepted for training.

The initial selection has to be tough, not only because of the need to identify technical potential but also because once a pilot is selected and trained, he will stay with the company, doing the same job, until retirement. It is unusual for a pilot to move to another airline during his career, and a move to another job within the airline (eg, manager or trainer) is regarded as a sideways move. A pilot is the *only* thing to be.

Initial Training

This is a period of stuctured courses lasting 14 months and involving a minimum of 200 hours flying experience. It is carried out at a commercial flying school approved by the Civil Aviation Authority under the jurisdiction of the Department of Transport.

At the end of this period I was awarded a Commercial Pilot's Licence and after additional experience, an Air Transport Pilot's Licence. I then joined the airline as a co-pilot, a status which will continue until I've completed a further period of six to nine years when I become a captain.

Continuing Professional Development

The Civil Aviation Authority sets standards for training and issues licences to pilots but takes no direct responsibility for CPD. The maintenance of standards is entirely the responsibility of the airline, which has set up a system of such vigour that there is almost no difference between doing the job and doing your CPD. It's part of the job, not an add-on. If you don't pass your frequent flying exams you lose your licence and you're out of the job. You have to demonstrate your competence to fly that particular plane; if you change the type of plane you pilot you have a whole new set of tests to pass.

The tests are carried out twice a year and take two days. You have to show that you understand the systems (a competency exam) and six months later you sit it again and also show that you can fly without visual reference (flying 'blind') using a simulator. Yearly, another pilot or training captain will sit in with you on a simulated routine trip to assess your 'cockpit resource management' (team work) and this is videoed and later reviewed.

After every 'exam' there is a long debriefing with both good points and development points identified. In addition, there is a 30 minute debriefing after every trip. The flight manager of the fleet takes the role of 'line manager' and, together with a training manager, will identify any action to be taken. Training captains, who are working pilots approved by the Civil Aviation Authority, also coach 'on the job' ie, on flights. Records of all of this are kept by the CAA and the training manager.

For more long-term development the airline has a scheme called 'Realising Flight Crew Potential' (RFCP) which can be used for development into managerial or trainer roles. I have recently been cleared to operate the flight simulator and to take on cadets. In the future I would like to take on a trainer role using schemes available.

Conclusions

The training and the maintenance of professional competence are second to none. There is a great deal of stress before the frequent exams but there is constant monitoring, feedback and support. Flying is 80 per cent routine, 15 per cent very difficult and 5 per cent critical. The quantity and quality of CPD which is provided means that I can manage it all with confidence.

THE ENGINEERING ACADEMIC's TALE

Introduction

I have been a mechanical engineer all my professional life and I have spent most of my working life in an academic environment. This has sometimes led to a slightly schizophrenic existence.

It means that I have to reconcile the demands of my profession with my employer's requirements, plus, of course, the demands and expectations I place upon myself. In addition, as an academic, I am committed to the development of new knowledge within my field and this adds yet a further layer to my CPD.

The essential nature of the CPD process in which I engage is that it is done almost entirely in an unsupervised way, requiring that I use my own initiative.

Professional Training and First Post

My original professional training followed a conventional route. I studied engineering at a redbrick university and became a member of the Institution of Mechanical Engineers (MIMechE) and a Chartered Engineer (C.Eng). Following this, I had a period in industry where there was no CPD requirement and was only involved in training required by the employer.

Current Post

Currently, I am a lecturer in a 1960s technological university where I am responsible for a number of areas in the work of the mechanical engineering department. These include direct responsibility for students (senior tutor, first year tutor) plus, most importantly, industrial tutor which includes arranging year placements in industry as the course is a 'thin sandwich'. This involves considerable follow-up work and visits to companies and so keeps me up-to-date on current industrial practices and developments.

My work with students has meant that I have had to keep current with information technology (word-processors, spreadsheets and the like) as well as the complex lab instruments which are driven by specialist software. There is no formal expectation that I should carry out this learning and it is driven by my own need to be better at what I do. I am totally self-taught in these areas and arrange training on my own initiative.

The university is developing a form of appraisal but it is at a fairly primitive stage and only involves agreeing a few goals which are monitored yearly. Essentially, I do what academics have always done, namely identifying my own training and development needs, discovering how they can be met and doing it.

The undergraduate course leads to membership of the professional body (Institution of Mechanical Engineers) and I liaise with them on behalf of the students on requirements for membership and standards and current developments in the profession. This, of course, is CPD 'on the hoof' for me and is invaluable as the Institution places no formal CPD requirements on members.

In order to keep up-to-date in my specialist field I read the relevant professional journals, publish and attend conferences. Academics are part of a world-wide community of specialists who communicate through journals and at conferences. In this way academics' CPD is intrinsically tied up with their work – there is no separation between one's academic work and one's CPD.

Conclusion

CPD and my working life are inextricably linked – I can't do one without the other. Whether it's the latest software or the most recent development in my field I *have* to do it. Nobody makes me, no one checks whether I do it. I just do it every day as naturally and easily as breathing.

THE FINANCIAL ADVISER'S TALE

First Jobs

I am a financial adviser and came into this field almost by accident. My first post was with Sony which I joined as an operative and progressed to team leader, negotiator and job evaluator. I took voluntary redundancy and began to study to become a solicitor but found that I couldn't get a grant to support me during my studies.

Into the Finance Industry

I was looking for a 'people-orientation' in my work and was attracted by an advertisement in *The Sunday Times* which showed the financial adviser as someone who helped people solve their financial problems. I am now able to provide this service, but in my first job I was locked into a system of cold calls, hard sell and commission only. Also, all I could provide to clients was that particular company's products.

I had no preconceptions about the work when I went into it. I also had no relevant skills. I had a brief period of product training but nothing else. I stayed one month but couldn't stand the predatory environment of the company. I had begun to appreciate and like the nature of the industry so decided to stay in it.

Next Financial Job

I took a post in the local branch of a national insurance company which offered not only initial training in products but also in-house meetings and workshops. The area manager placed an emphasis upon professional development and recommended that I should spend a minimum of one hour a day studying the industry. This meant unstructured CPD through reading the financial press and published reports. Later, I was sent on external courses in selling, marketing and interpersonal skills.

I picked the brains of everyone and brought client problems for analysis. I particularly valued the advice and support of more experienced colleagues who often acted as mentors. I built a network of external experts and began to study for the Financial Planning Certificate of the Chartered Insurance Institute. Currently, I have passed Part 1 and should have completed all three parts by 1995, making me a full member.

After two years I realized I needed to become an independent adviser so that I wasn't tied to a single range of products but had a free choice. I joined a company of independent financial consultants in the City.

Being Independent

The group shares facilities but in every other respect each consultant is independent. The investment which I have to make in my own learning means that CPD has become inextricably linked to the job. Because of the breadth, depth and complexity of the financial world and the constantly changing legislation on tax and financial services as well as changing markets, keeping up to date and aware is an obligatory requirement for CPD.

This includes exchanging information with colleagues about products and solutions, meetings with insurance and investment analysts, reading periodicals, books and newspapers, attending courses and seminars, product analysis and developing sources of information. There is a points system which credits both structured and unstructured CPD as well as professional exams. In the organization there is a compliance manager who monitors everyone's CPD.

CPD has become a major part of my business activity. Although there is a requirement to carry out CPD, I do far more than is laid down so that I can be completely competent and provide a fully professional service to my clients. In a highly saturated market, this is the only way to distinguish oneself from the competition and offer a value-added service.

THE IT CONSULTANT'S TALE

Early Days

I studied English at Oxford University and followed this with a teacher training qualification. I then worked in Rudolf Steiner schools. The major vehicle for my personal and professional development at this time was the weekly learning meetings which were held for all staff.

After five years, I realized that I felt as if I'd been living in schools all my life and needed more adult interactions in my professional life.

Next Steps

By that time I was married and had children and, although I didn't want to teach, I certainly needed a job which would support both me and my family. I needed one which would recognize capacity without specific knowledge as my experience was limited to teaching. I chose to enter the computer industry as a salesman, working for a subsidiary of ICL which sold supplies to computer installations.

I was given four days training in selling and on the fourth day I was on the road. Within a year I was offered the role of company sales trainer and a fast track management path to the board but decided I'd learnt everything I could learn there and needed to move to IBM where I could learn more. There, I was given one year's training which included three months classroom tuition, coaching, and the enormous benefit of no selling quota. This enabled me to concentrate upon learning without the anxiety and pressure of a sales target.

Maintenance of competence was assured by two weeks of workshops and training a year which broadened learning to include how the business worked and solving people's problems.

After four years with IBM I felt that the company was walking away from their core values of service and respect for the individual. It was time to move on.

Moving On

I then joined a small software company which became the UK market leader in application software for IBM mid-range systems. I was given the post of director, southern region. In this company, every client was regarded as a new situation, and every situation a learning opportunity. Part of my job was to coach and develop the managers and I set up workshops and internal management training as well as informal on-the-job coaching.

Eventually, I was invited by an advertising agency to form a company to operate its computing interests. When I joined, the company was operating with a loss equal to its modest turnover. In three years its turnover was £7.4 million with an operating profit of £650,000, and the company was a market leader.

I had learnt from the inside of businesses how to make them successful. My next step was to discover how to do that working from the outside. In 1991 I formed my own consultancy for the design and implementation of change, which is a centre for innovative thought, process facilitation and workshops, on most aspects of organization development and marketing.

Ways of Learning

Having reviewed my work-related experiences I can see that there has been a pattern of learning that has gradually developed. I categorize these as follows:

- Thinking – about what I know, writing about it, designing and running workshops on it, giving talks and seminars, reading and attending workshops to get input. The key thing is to identify the question for me and for the client (what's going on?) and work with it, both inwardly and outwardly.
- Doing – taking on new things – finding out how to do them, working at the cross-over points, eg, marketing plus IT may lead to an organization development issue.

- Meeting – sharing experiences with my networks helps me develop and process ideas, identify the questions that are at the heart of problem and, importantly, my wife is a source of insights and the way to a more balanced view.

Being involved in personal development is, for me, central to my professional development. The two go hand-in-hand and I enjoy taking them seriously.

THE LIBRARIAN'S TALE

Beginnings

I began work in the public library system at the age of 16 and started to study part-time for the Library Association's professional exams. After three to four years of part-time study and one year in full time study, I had passed many papers several times but not in the right combination. In all, it took me ten years to achieve full Chartered Librarian status. The lesson I learned from this was, 'Stick with it!', a maxim that should be the motto of everyone pursuing professional qualifications in their own time.

Starting Teaching

I found that my commitment to the excitement of library work led me to an interest in staff development. I wanted to train more people to enjoy working in libraries. I was accepted for a lecturing post in a polytechnic where I taught in a Library School (now the Department of Library Information Studies).

As I was in an academic environment as well as tutoring I had to learn a whole new set of skills relating to research and writing. It was really a 'seat of the pants' or trial and error professional development process. Inevitably, a lifetime's experience of libraries gave me a head start. I was so familiar with using libraries that the move from vocational study to academic research and writing was relatively painless. Because I have always operated in libraries, informal, unstructured CPD has always been available to me and has become part of my way of working.

Redundancy meant I left the poly and picked up a two-year research contract (more skills to develop). Then I was employed by the librarians' professional body, the Library Association, to organize continuing education. Over a six-year period I created a coherent programme of CPD events and was responsible for setting up a CPD scheme for all members.

The CPD Scheme

This is called 'The Framework for Continuing Professional Development' and consists of a complementary set of guidelines for individuals and employers. It is presented in the form of a planning cycle which goes through six stages from present job/future roles/personal priorities to the record of achievement and review of priorities. The librarian/information professional is encouraged to design the plan in consultation with the employer. The principles underlying the scheme are that it is a working document for the individual to use to plan, record and monitor progress.

The voluntary scheme involves each individual taking responsibility for their own CPD in partnership with their employer.

Conclusions

There has been no separation between my professional development and my CPD. It seems that since my teens I have been carrying out CPD as regularly as I go to work – the two are inseparable either through informal, unstructured learning or, early in my career, for qualifications. Study is almost a way of life. As I regard the prospect of early retirement and a new career as an independent consultant, I can see the pattern continuing.

THE PERSONNEL PROFESSIONAL'S TALE

First Jobs

After I left school at 16 with four 'O' levels I attended the local technical college and took an OND in business studies. Although I had no experience or qualifications in office work my first post was as personal assistant to a manager. As I had neither shorthand nor typing qualifications I suppose I must have got the post through sheer cheek. I soon took some evening classes in typing and shorthand and became acceptably competent.

I survived that experience and it confirmed my view that I was not going to spend my life in a traditional woman's role as an office 'helper'. Nevertheless, my next post was as a secretary in a personnel department where I more or less did the personnel officer's job. There were no training opportunities but I became aware of of the possibility of becoming a personnel professional by taking the Institute of Personnel Management (IPM, as it then was) exams. My boss refused to support me in this as 'you don't need it in this job'.

First Professional Qualification

I then married and spent a period in temporary jobs as I followed my husband around the country. Eventually we settled in the Thames Valley and I got a job as a recruitment consultant. I was, of course, not really qualified to do this, but the company provided in-house training. Once again, I had started a job without any real qualifications to do it and acquired the skills later – not an ideal way to develop competence, but one which seemed to work for me at that stage of my life.

As I was now determined to gain the IPM qualification I made sure that my next post as a personnel officer included a half day's 'day release' to study and quickly became an AIPM (Associate of the IPM). I eventually left the job to have a baby but was able to upgrade my AIPM to MIPM (Member of the IPM) by presenting evidence of relevant work experience.

I also started to study for a Masters degree in industrial relations and discovered the area of work called 'management consultancy'. This suited my domestic circumstances very well and I started to work as an independent consultant. This included teaching in further and higher education, although I had no formal teaching qualification or experience. At this time I became involved in a women returners' course at a local university and I realized I had found my career direction.

My Current CPD

I now work with a business partner on courses which are funded by the European Social Fund (ESF).

My CPD is provided in two ways: mainly through my own efforts and through my professional body, the IPD (formerly the IPM). I have created a network of contacts, primarily women involved in some aspect of women's courses or who are independent consultants themselves. Together with my business partner I have created a body called the Women's Development Forum which provides both support and stimulation for its members. The creation, maintenance and utilization of this Forum has been my primary CPD activity for the last two years.

In addition, the IPD provides journals and branch meetings which keep me in touch with other personnel professionals. The institute's IPD scheme focuses upon learning: recording, recognizing and reflecting on what you do and what it means. The scheme states: 'The most important aspect of CPD is the learning outcome, not the precise amount of input'.

A minimum level of five days or 30 hours of study per annum is recommended, with a probable future requirement of CPD evidence for upgrading. However, most of the approved activities would only realistically be available to members in large companies and this is likely to exclude or be difficult for certain categories of members such as the self-employed and people taking a career break.

Summary

Preparing this CPD history has enabled me to reflect upon the process of getting to where I am now and the part CPD has played. Although I haven't always called it CPD it has played a central role in my personal and professional development and I suppose it's really that old friend, lifelong learning, in a more formal guise. Although the professional body supports me in some respects, it is primarily what I identify as my own personal and professional needs and how I meet them which have the greatest benefit. The formal scheme gives me a structure, a discipline and a framework within which to plan.

THE PSYCHOTHERAPIST'S TALE

First Jobs

Following 'A' levels I spent four years at the Department of Employment carrying out recruitment interviewing for which I was given brief training. I moved to the Michelin Tyre Company where I was involved in more sophisticated recruitment methods including assessment centres. This led to the management fast track programme and more involvement in psychometric testing for which I was given professional training. I was then promoted to be management training officer.

First Management Posts

I moved to the Smiths Food Group as assistant to the group personnel manager, with wide responsiblities. I studied and got the Institute of Personnel Managers qualification (IPM) and the Institute of Training and Development (ITD) Diploma in Training Management. I moved to a job as recruitment manager in a local authority with 10,500 staff and continued to take numerous short courses in my own time as well as at work. The work-based courses were very specifically related to my job, eg 'Equal Opportunities in the Inner Cities' and kept me up-to-date on legislation and new areas of responsibility.

Going Independent

In 1987 I left the local authority and became a consultancy manager with a networking consultancy which provided ground breaking personal empowerment, stress management, counselling and transition management training to both private and public sector clients. In 1989 I started my own consultancy.

I had now entered a period of intensive attendance at courses of study which would equip me for my role as a consultant. During the following years (and continuing to the present) I became skilled and professionally qualified in a number of new areas, including master practitioner in neuro-linguistic programming (NLP), time line therapist, registered consultant with the IPD, and BPS-registered psychometric tester.

Observations on my CPD

My career has taken some interesting twists and turns. From the first job doing recruitment interviews for the Department of Employment to my present consultancy practice, CPD has been my inspiration and support in every new venture in my professional life.

THE SELF-EMPLOYED ACCOUNTING TECHNICIAN'S TALE

The Start

I left school with six 'O' levels and worked in various clerical positions for over 13 years. It soon became clear that if I wanted to improve my career prospects I needed to acquire some qualifications. I attended a government-funded TOPS course at a local college as a mature student which led to study for the Institute of Accounting Technicians qualification (later re-named the Association of Accounting Technicians). At the same time, I passed two 'A' levels.

First Professional Position

I then moved from Wales to London and took my first post-qualification job as an audit/accounts clerk where I stayed for 12 years. The firm had an appraisal system which was related primarily to pay rather than performance. Professional development was not individually focused but concentrated mainly on technical updating for all staff. There was also some interpersonal skills training but the primary focus was on developing business skills.

It was not until a training consortium was set up by a group of local accountancy practices, of which my firm was a founder member, eight years after I joined the practice, that there was any form of training. Prior to that, training was minimal. The only way staff could update their skills was to study for additional qualifications – a route that I chose to take, becoming a part-qualified Certified Accountant.

The training consortium concentrated upon two main areas: audit legislation and financial reporting requirements necessary for junior and inexperienced staff. All staff and partners had training by the consortium at the level appropriate for the position. There was no identification of individual training and development needs, but it was recognized that everyone had to keep up-to-date on changing legislation. It was the partners alone who decided on the most appropriate courses.

In my next firm there was no direct training provided but a programme of courses was issued by an accountancy consortium. The decision about the courses for me to attend was taken jointly by me and one of the partners. Again, there was constant up-dating plus some interpersonal skills training but there was no assessment of individual training needs.

During this period I was not involved in formal CPD linked to a professional body. All training and development was linked to particular job-related skills.

Next Posts

I then moved to a much smaller accountancy practice which also used the same training consortium, so I continued to attend some courses. However, in practice, because of pressure of work it was very difficult to maintain my professional standards by attending courses and seminars – I didn't attend as many as I should.

Going Self-Employed

For the last ten months I have been self-employed. This means that I am now responsible for my own CPD. The sources for this are of four kinds:

- my professional body – The Association of Accounting Technicians (AAT)
- courses and seminars offered by the training consortium
- informal support groups
- my own assessment of needs and actions to meet them.

When I started my business I began by attending courses for the newly self-employed provided by the local Training and Enterprise Council (TEC). This enabled me to learn how to set myself up professionally. The courses included marketing, customer relations and other skills which I had not previously needed.

My professional body, the AAT, is in the process of refining and developing their CPD provision, so it has not been too relevant so far. The training consortium courses and seminars provide me with the means of keeping up-to-date and I supplement this with reading professional journals and manuals.

I attend meetings of business groups, including the local Chamber of Commerce, businesswomen's clubs and other small business groups. These provide me with stimulation, new ideas and sometimes new clients! Together, they reduce the isolation of working alone.

It is particularly important for me to maintain and develop my expertise as my reputation and the success of my business largely depends upon it. Although it involves both time and money it is a price I am willing to pay.

THE SOLICITOR'S TALE

Preparation to Enter the Practice of Law

I took a law degree at Cambridge University and followed this with six months at the College of Law (a Law Society-run Institute) where I took Part 2 of the Law Society's examinations. I spent a further two years in Articles with a law firm in the City of London and after that was admitted as a solicitor.

Current Post

On qualification, I moved from the firm where I had been articled and joined a smaller firm as an assistant solicitor, then as a salaried partner in the practice and now as an equity partner (owner status).

Part of my responsibility in this post is that of the training partner. This means that not only am I responsible for my own CPD but also that of the junior solicitors. In practice, this means that it is assumed that each solicitor has knowledge of the scheme and its requirements and that it is their own responsibility to comply. My activity in this respect is limited to collating the courses available and keeping attendance records. In effect, I rubber-stamp their attendance.

Selection of Suitable CPD Activities

The firm is organized in specialist departments, each of which identifies suitable courses from the Law Society-approved courses available from various course suppliers. From this list, junior solicitors agree with their supervising partner the choice of courses to attend and report back how useful and relevant it was to them and the needs of the practice.

Informal appraisal of performance is carried out by the partners using a single criterion of success: has the fee-earning capacity of the individual been enhanced and how can it be further improved?

Formal appraisal systems and the identification of individual training and development needs are planned for the future but currently there are no individual Personal Development Plans prepared other than as a part of the present informal appraisal system. There is no element of personal development. The Law Society lays down what must be done and there is a clear focus upon areas relevant to fee-earning activities. The emphasis is upon legal content plus some professional skills courses.

There are some difficulties in finding courses which are at the right level. Most courses are provided by tried and trusted providers but updating at the right level may be hard to find. This means that the whole process can be very costly for an individual firm.

The Scheme

In 1977 the Council of the Society reported to the Royal Commission on Legal Services that:

> The Law Society regards continuing education (CE) as a most important tool with which to improve the standards and competence of the profession and to enable it to meet the changing demands of society in the future and it sees the provision of a comprehensive system of CE as one of its most urgent tasks.

Following this, a CE scheme was introduced in 1985 and revised at intervals until the current scheme was introduced in 1992. It is called CPD and there are precise requirements laid down at different career stages and for different professional and personal circumstances (eg, 'not in law related employment' or working part-time).

Participation is mandatory, although this word is not used in the rubric of the scheme, and requirements can be met through a variety of methods. Attendance at accredited courses is particularly favoured (up to 100 but a minimum of 25 per cent attendance at courses), and also includes workshops and distance learning.

My own CPD

In addition to fulfilling the formal requirements laid down by the scheme, I always read the *Law Society Gazette* and other legal periodicals, particularly noting updating articles, case reports and courses on them. In addition, we have an Internal Update – a colleague scans the legal press and circulates important articles.

Although any scheme could be improved, it seems to me that the Law Society scheme works very well and ensures professional updating.

THE SURVEYOR'S TALE

Entry to the Profession

I have been in surveying since I became an articled pupil in 1966. Entry to the profession was relatively easy at that time and I could get direct entry through the College of Estate Management exams which were run by the Institute of Surveying. Now, entry to the profession is by accredited degree with a final period of rigorous assessment lasting two to three years.

I achieved election to Associateship in 1969. The two Institutes merged in 1970 to become the Royal Institution of Chartered Surveyors and I have been a practising Chartered Surveyer ever since.

Branch Activities

Much of my CPD is carried out through the local branch of which I am secretary. The branch has more than 3,500 members and we carry out a wide variety of activities, including regular meetings, a quarterly newsletter and a conference which gets bigger and more successful each year.

I have been particularly active on the branch committee arranging the programme of events and I regard my role as secretary of the branch as a particularly important part of my own CPD. There is no CPD sub-committee which could help branch members with their CPD and we don't design the programme with CPD in mind. Nevertheless, the effect of what we do as a branch is to provide the opportunity for CPD-related activities. The divisional committee acts as a CPD committee. Members don't ask for help, but the combined effect of the programme and the newsletter is to keep members aware of changes that are taking place in the profession.

The CPD Scheme

Under the Royal Charter the Institution is charged with the responsibility to '... maintain and promote the usefulness of the profession for the public advantage'.

The regulations made by the general council describe CPD as:

the systematic maintenance, improvement and broadening of knowledge and skill and the development of personal qualities necessary for the execution of professional and technical duties throughout the practitioner's working life.

Members are responsible for keeping a record of their participation in qualifying activities. The attendance requirement for Professional Associates and Fellows is a minimum of 60 hours in every consecutive period of three years. These activities could include courses, conferences, structured reading, distance learning, authorship, study and research.

To qualify as CPD, an activity must be related to some part of the theory and practice of surveying as defined in the Royal Charter, other technical topics or personal and business skills designed to increase a member's management or business efficiency.

Personal Conclusion

I have always found that my CPD activity has been a great source of both personal and professional development. Of course the formal activities plus regular reading of journals and reports keep me up-to-date. But over and above that, the informal contacts, whether it's a RICS committee or a meeting after work with other surveyors means that I maintain my network of contacts and I keep my finger on the pulse of the profession both locally and nationally.

THE TEACHER'S TALE

How it Started

My story opens with a situation that is very typical of young people: enrolling for a course of study and leaving after the first year, only in my case it was all rather ironic as the course of study I abandoned at 19 later became my lifelong career path – a teacher.

First Jobs

I married, had two children and taught unqualified for six years. Eventually, changes in the regulations for teaching meant that I trained for three years and became a qualified primary school teacher. I taught for 20 years and attended at least two or three INSET (In-service Education and Training) courses a year. However, this did not mean that I had a 'career' – nobody was linking my choice of courses to any kind of plan. INSET courses were entirely concerned with enhancing your current competence as you judged your need, and when you got back to school after a course there was no follow-up.

I eventually reached the dizzy heights of deputy head, and pretty well ran the school myself. I also realized that I needed to change my career direction as it was virtually impossible to achieve a headship through legitimate channels – only selected 'favourites' were chosen.

My Career Takes Off

I identified more courses I wanted to attend and persuaded the head to release funds for this. He made it unpleasant and difficult for me but could do little to prevent me.

I had got the studying bug and decided that I wanted to do a Masters degree, but the head didn't allow this and actively discouraged professional development. Off my own bat I studied for two degree-equivalent courses which I attended part-time and paid for myself.

The Next Steps

By this time I had given up on that school and head and took a peripatetic 'problem-solving' role which took me into a number of different schools in the area. My studies had developed my expertise in counselling, dysfunctional families and supporting school heads and staff through difficult problems. I continued to study, specializing in developing training in counselling and related skills.

The advisory team of which I was a part was disbanded and I was offered early retirement. This enabled me to leave teaching and set up as an independent consultant specializing in personal development. I had been aware for some time that I would be leaving the local education authority and five years earlier had begun to build my 'escape tunnel'. I wasn't sure what it would look like or when it would be needed, but I embarked on an intensive programme of self-development which continues to this day. Ironically, when I left the authority I was inundated with offers of headships which hadn't been available when I might have been happy to accept.

Current Position

I continue with my increasingly successful business. I also continue to study and have signed up with the Open University for an MA of which I am in the final stages. I also have membership of the British Association of Counsellors (BAC) and its American equivalent, BACA, have membership of the Institute of Training and Development (now the IPD) and have accreditation and membership of the College of Preceptors and the Institute of Stress Management.

My personal and professional development has been (and continues to be) my inspiration and the motor which drives my professional life.

THE WOMAN RETURNER'S TALE

First Qualifications

I am a General Practitioner. I qualified as doctor with a BSc MBChB from Glasgow University and followed this with a preregistration year in hospital.

We junior doctors were all thrown in at the deep end with little or no support from senior staff, but with a heavy workload and serious responsibilities. The only CPD I had during this period came through experiential learning, but this was not guided, supported or reviewed by seniors. All the junior doctors supported each other and we learnt together, but this was completely informal and unstructured.

In addition, there was no system of review and assessment at the end of your year in hospital. If you survived the year without making any major errors you emerged qualified to practise. In summary, the professional development during this period was entirely informal and *ad hoc*.

First Jobs

My general practice training involved a minimum of three years in various specialities with six-month blocks in hospitals and general practice. At the end, I was awarded the Vocational Training Scheme Certificate. During this period I was supported by a regular tutor called a 'GP trainer' who also assssed my development. I then took a year out and worked abroad as a locum (a temporary replacement doctor).

I returned to the UK, got married and worked as a 'permanent' locum for one and a half years. I attended teaching sessions organized by the postgraduate (PG) centre at the local hospital which publishes a list of lecture sessions on topics such as new drugs. In addition, I had a network of other young doctors who had trained with me to help me with advice and information.

The Move to the South

I now entered a critical phase in my professional life. I had left behind my peer group in Glasgow and began to look for suitable doctors' partnerships who would employ me. I had no network of contacts as I'd had in Glasgow so it was difficult to find locum work. The local PG centre was not very helpful and the BMA didn't provide any central register of vacancies. I didn't want a great deal of work but wanted to establish contacts in the area.

I then became pregnant, took a year and a half out and then had a new role: 'qualified doctor with young child seeks locum work'. I'd just spent nearly ten years becoming qualified and experienced and I wasn't about to waste it.

Qualified Doctor with Small Child

I returned to work when my son was a year old and did this by enrolling on the Doctor's Retainer Scheme. This scheme enables returners to work an agreed number of sessions either in hospital or general practice in order to keep in contact and up-to-date. It's available for everyone who takes a career break but is primarily used by mothers of young children.

Notionally, there is a district tutor – to keep an eye on your career development during this period and tackle any problems which might arise. However, the reality is that the district tutor is a busy GP who has little incentive to give the doctors on the scheme much attention.

The CPD requirement is that you attend seven 'educational' sessions (courses) per year from a list issued by the local PG centre. No one reviews the appropriateness of the courses you have chosen and the only record that is kept is 'signing in' and attendance is optional.

The cost of courses is high and as session (ie, part-time) work is badly paid, this makes attendance difficult. In addition, most meetings are held in the evening which usually precludes attendance by mothers of young children.

I am currently seeking out the local Women Practioners Group and the Young Practitioners Group, which could give me support.

Conclusions

After a long and expensive investment in my professional development as a doctor I am now, as a young mother, finding it almost impossible to maintain the standards necessary. Women doctors have a special contribution to make to the health service and to individual patients but a new approach is needed which takes account of their circumstances.

16

The Way Ahead

Sandra Clyne

INTRODUCTION

The book has covered a lot of ground and shown a number of aspects of CPD as it is currently practised. Professions and occupations, both traditional and new, have been examined, as well as the role of professional bodies and the individual professional – the point and focus of CPD.

Is it possible to summarize or draw conclusions about future directions in CPD? Are there any lessons to be learnt or useful truths to be noted which can be built upon for the future and give pointers to the way ahead? These questions will be considered in this section.

ISSUES RAISED

A number of themes and trends in the current state of CPD have emerged. Chief among these is the rapid and increasing pace of *change*, which is affecting all professions. Also notable is the rise of new professions and occupations which would like to join the ranks of the established professionals, and who see CPD as a way to advance their cause. This last trend is one clear new development.

One new occupation which is affecting professionals is the emergence of the information technology specialist.

This development means that professionals have to master a whole new area of skills, computer literacy being a requirement for all professionals, however distant this is from their original discipline and specialism.

Employers are becoming increasingly involved in CPD, realizing that CPD needs to be closely linked to training and staff development plans and integrated with them.

The requirement for professionals to be skilled in business management also lays a new emphasis upon an area of CPD familiar to small partnerships but which is being extended to more professionals as many set themselves up in self-employment or in a new business-focused role with a traditional employer, eg the NHS. The final element is the development of management itself as a new profession through the system of NVQs in management: a potential new area for CPD.

New patterns of employment mean that the lone professional, or one in partnership with a small group, will increase. IT will play a key part in this, enabling the professional to use both informal networking and the Internet to keep in contact with partners and professionals worldwide.

The implications of the above for the development of CPD practice can be gauged by reference to the following factors:

- the importance of information technology
- the integration of CPD into the business planning of organizations, which has the potential to give the professional more influence
- the developing professionalism of the manager, which can be added to existing professional qualifications to make the role of the professional more central to the business
- the self-employed professional, able to maintain contact with peers using various forms of networking; again, a new area of learning

The second key theme which has arisen is that of the *individual* professional. The book has presented a number of approaches and methods of improving learning effectiveness. Many professionals are highly motivated, self-reliant and creative in designing their CPD and there are many new approaches available. Realistically, most professionals will be attending courses and conferences, some of which will be in new areas (IT, for example) but most will continue to do what they've always done – using the tried and tested methods which keep them up to date and in touch with their profession.

Probably the most exciting new development and one which is likely to have the greatest effect is the development and use of personal development plans. PDPs are adaptable, and thus appropriate to professionals working in a variety of environments. They can be used by a large employer to link with appraisal. For a small practice, they can be used to identify learning for the individual and in the group. The self-employed professional can use a PDP to track progress and identify development needs.

CPD has the potential to be the driving force for the professions in maintaining and improving their status and position, as well as improving individual effectiveness. However, this positive view of CPD is not held by all professionals. Many of those interviewed for the research reported in Chapter 15 expressed negative views about CPD. The strength of these views ranged from the luke-warm to the downright cynical or even angry, and many regarded it as an imposition. This group will almost certainly fail to embrace the spirit of CPD, even if they go along with its practice.

The question then is: does it matter? As long as the minimum requirement is carried out, why is it necessary to do more? There are questions about CPD implicit in a number of contributions to this book, questions described by Andrew Gibbons as 'CPD Dilemmas'.

CPD DILEMMAS

CPD dilemmas take the form of opposing choices in CPD practice. They offer two different views on how CPD could be managed. The pairs of choices are:

- prescriptive structure – 'this is what you do', *or* free choice
- must be done *or* leave it up to you
- focus on learning inputs *or* focus on learning outcomes
- left to get on with it *or* supported
- trusted to do it *or* monitored
- educated and informed *or* coerced
- work/professional focus only *or* personal development is legitimate
- scheme that focuses on benefits and competence *or* scheme that emphasizes administrative convenience
- if you don't do it there are no penalties *or* if you don't do it there are penalties
- everything decided centrally *or* wide consultation with membership.

The central issues raised in the above are:

Who's in charge of CPD?

Who owns CPD?

and also

For whose benefit does CPD exist?

This raises some fundamental questions about the future role of CPD and the relationship between the professional bodies and the members. There are no fixed answers to the dilemmas shown above – they demonstrate that CPD is in a continuous state of review and reflection around these questions. Both professional bodies and members have to decide where they stand at any moment, realizing that dynamic CPD is continually redefining itself in the light of experience drawn from practice. It may be that all kinds of new forms of professionalism and matching CPD are developing quietly as new professions evolve and that the global changes are matched by the evolution of new forms of professional and related CPD.

In the meantime, this book has shown how professionals strive to be as good as possible at what they do, highlighting the role played by CPD in this process.

Appendix

The UK Inter-professional Group Survey of Continuing Professional Development Policy and Practice

SECTION 1: OVERVIEW

Introduction

The UK Inter-professional Group, represented by 17 members, acts as a forum to promote the professions and to exchange information on common issues. In 1992 the group surveyed members' policies on Continuing Professional Development (CPD). In recognition of the increasing importance of CPD, a working group was established in 1993 to conduct a detailed survey of CPD policies, activities and issues. The group held six meetings at which there were presentations and discussions of key issues. The information obtained from the professional associations which contributed has been collated by a researcher from Bristol University into this survey report.

The review, below, summarizes the main issues. Further details can be found in the survey responses which are reproduced in the second section of this report. Section three deals with the hopes and fears for the future of CPD.

The survey results show a number of common trends in CPD policy and practice concerning the motivation for introducing a CPD policy, leading to the adoption of either a voluntary or a compulsory policy, and in turn influencing the means through which the policy is pursued by the professional associations

Motivation for CPD

The position of the professional associations as regulatory bodies and guardians of standards strongly influences their approach to CPD policy and practice. The Royal College of Veterinary Surgeons (RCVS) has identified three motives for CPD: to main-

204

tain competence; to learn new skills and knowledge and to *retain public confidence.*

A number of other professional associations have indicated the same purpose in establishing CPD programmes; CPD is being promoted as the tool to show the public that standards are being met and maintained.

Voluntary/obligatory/compulsory

- *Voluntary* – a practitioner is free to choose whether or not to update.
- *Obligatory* – a practitioner is obliged to update by an ethical requirement in the profession's code of conduct. Alternatively, several institutions make CPD obligatory by a byelaw, rule or regulation.
- *Compulsory/mandatory* – a practitioner will be disbarred if he or she does not update. Professional byelaws include explicit references to CPD.

The decision to adopt a compulsory rather than a voluntary policy is part of the motivation to uphold standards and quality. More pragmatically, the decision may also be influenced by the source of funding. Employers/practices can claim expenditure on CPD as a trading expense whether or not it is required by an employee's professional association. The need for indemnity insurance may be a further motivation for adopting a compulsory approach.

The debate over whether or not a policy should be voluntary (benefits) or compulsory (sanctions) has dominated discussions about CPD. There are advantages and disadvantages to each system (Madden and Mitchell, 1993) and there may be regulatory reasons why particular professions choose the voluntary or compulsory route. There does not seem, however, to be an automatic correlation between the regulatory role and the adoption of a mandatory CPD policy: the European Patent Institute is a mandatory body but it has not introduced a compulsory CPD policy.

Promotion of CPD

The promotional activities undertaken by the professional associations are dependent on their approaches to CPD. A number of examples of good practice were shown in the survey. These include:

- methods of provision: several of the health professions and

architecture are developing distance learning and computer-aided CPD packages;
- guidance for practitioners: the pharmacists have issued formal guidance on CPD. Several engineering institutions issue a professional development record binder; The Engineering Council issues a career manager document;
- guidance for providers: the architects are planning a 'Providers' forum'; the pharmacists have produced a continuing education syllabus and a code of practice for providers; psychologists accredit courses, allowing providers to use the British Psychological Society symbol;
- assessment of performance: the dentists have established a peer review system and hope to introduce a clinical audit akin to the doctors';
- incentives: dentists are paid for participation in CPD; the pharmacists hope to introduce a postgraduate education allowance payable to individuals.

The hopes and fears of the professional associations show more clearly the UK trends in CPD. The most common fears were:

- the low levels of funding for CPD and uncertainty about continued funding;
- the maintenance of quality and the burden of administrative time in quality assessment.
- assessment measures imposed from outside the profession;
- the lack of motivation amongst practitioners, due to time pressure and lack of funding and support from employers;
- if CPD becomes mandatory, it risks becoming a chore;
- if CPD becomes voluntary, it risks becoming low priority;
- the introduction of a threshold professional model related to skill level assessment.

The most common hopes were:

- an increase in funding and an expansion of the CPD system;
- greater motivation on the part of practitioners, employers and funding bodies;
- a diversification in the delivery methods for CPD;
- the establishment of CPD as an acceptable concept for the professions, just as initial qualifications have been accepted.

Reference

Madden, CA and Mitchell, VA (1993) *Professions, Standards and Competence*, University of Bristol.

SECTION 2: SURVEY RESULTS

Table A.1 *Professional bodies examined in this survey*

Statutory/Chartered Institution	Membership	CPD Status	Minimum CPD per annum	Guidance and promotion
Health				
General Medical Council	187,696	Compulsory and Obligatory	Clinical audit	Regional postgraduate deans/Royal Colleges
Royal Pharmaceutical Society of Great Britain	39,443	Obligatory	30 hours	National and regional tutors National CE syllabus
General Dental Council	27,068	Obligatory		Regional advisers
Chartered Society of Physiotherapists	24,000	Voluntary		Regional boards and branches
General Optical Council	6,800	Mandatory for student supervisors Obligatory		Regional societies Distance learning
British Psychological Society	7,278	Obligatory		
Royal College of Veterinary Surgeons	14,220	Obligatory		
Engineering				
Institution of Electrical Engineers	52,817	Obligatory		Career helpline Professional brief Career development Database info
Institution of Mechanical Engineers	46,632	Voluntary	50 hours	
Institute of Marine Engineering	10,430	Voluntary		Leaflet on career development programme
Institute of Chemical Engineering	8,619	Voluntary		
Institution of Mining Engineers	1,910	Voluntary		
Construction				
Royal Institution of Chartered Surveyors	90,576	Obligatory	20 hours (60 hrs in 3 yrs)	Distance learning
Institution of Civil Engineers	48,185	Obligatory	5 days per year	Personal development plan
Royal Institute of British Architects	28,000	Obligatory	35 hours	Personal development plan

Statutory/Chartered Institution	Membership	CPD Status	Minimum CPD per annum	Guidance and promotion
Construction continued				
Institution of Structural Engineers	9,168	Obligatory	20 hours	Career planner and Diary CPD Handbook
Royal Town Planning Institute	18,000	Obligatory	50 hrs in 2 years	CPD personal record Practice advice note
Accountancy and Financial Services				
Institute of Chartered Accountants in England and Wales	104,559	Compulsory for some categories	150 points per yr 3 points for structured, 1 for unstructured	CPE record and guide lines TV station
Insurance and Financial Services	8,000	Compulsory for chartered	180 points over 3 yrs; min 50 per year	Information and guidance to be produced, 1/1/95
Institute of Actuaries	4,861	Compulsory for some categories	15 hours per yr formal activity, 52 hrs informal	Members' handbook
Legal				
The Law Society for England and Wales (refers only to solicitors)	75,000 members 57,000 practising	Compulsory	Up to 4th yr, 16 hrs per yr From 4th year on, post-admission training a minimum of 48 hrs over 3 years	Training Record; network of local Law Societies, some have Education committees
Chartered Institute of Patent Agents	1,282	Voluntary		

A summary of the results for each professional sector is shown below, with detailed information on each profession in Section 2.

Table A.2 *Professions examined in this survey*

Health	Engineering	Construction	Financial Services	Legal
Dentistry	Chemical Eng	Architecture	Accountancy	Law
Medicine	Electrical Eng	Civil Eng	Actuarial	Patent Agency
Optometry	Marine Eng	Structural Eng	Insurance and Financial Services	
Pharmacy	Mechanical Eng	Surveying		
Physiotherapy	Mining Eng	Town Planning		
Psychology				
Veterinary Surgery				

Summary

Health

CPD requirements in the health sector range from statutorily defined to ethically required:

- Doctors have a *mandatory* requirement to update; those employed by the NHS are required to take part in clinical audits. In general, doctors have an ethical requirement to update;
- dentists are in the process of reviewing CPD arrangements. In the meantime, their notes of guidance *recommend* CPD;
- psychologists have a *voluntary* system, but CPD is *required* for renewal of the Practising Certificate;
- optometrists will introduce an *obligatory* system in the future. In the meantime, CPD is only *mandatory* for supervisors of pre-registration students;
- veterinary surgeons are *ethically required* to update;
- pharmacists have a professional obligation under the terms of their code of ethics. Like the optometrists, CPD is mandatory for tutors of pre-registration trainees.

The requirement for a CPD record ranged from voluntary to none. *Sanctions* can be invoked in two cases, in the professions of optometry and psychology.

Engineering

Individual engineering institutes have varying approaches to minimum attendance:

- IMechE requires minimum attendance;
- IMarE, IChemE and IMinE maintain *voluntary* systems;
- IChemE is awaiting the outcome of a review to introduce a *sanctions* policy. Otherwise, a breach of the code of professional conduct may lead to disciplinary action.

Construction

The professional associations in the CPD in Construction Group all maintain an *obligatory* policy and stipulate a minimum amount of time spent in CPD ranging from 20 hours (60 hours over three years) at the Royal Institution of Chartered Surveyors to 20 hours at the Institution of Structural Engineers.

The Royal Institute of British Architects *recommends* that practitioners should endeavour to take part in additional CPD on top of the *obligatory* minimum of 35 hours.

Financial Services

- Accountants are *recommended* to undertake minimum attendance, some categories are *obliged*;
- insurance practitioners are *obliged* in order to reach chartered status;
- appointed actuaries and insurance advisers operate an *obligatory* attendance system; other actuaries may attend *voluntarily*.

Removal of the chartered title exists as a sanction in the insurance and actuarial professions.

Legal

- the legal profession *requires* minimum attendance;
- patent agents operate a *voluntary* system.

Sanctions apply to both professions in this category. Removal of the chartered title exists as a possible sanction. There is some evidence of difficulty in applying harsh sanctions in the legal profession.

SECTION 3: DETAILED INFORMATION FOR EACH PROFESSION

Profession: **Accountancy**

Regulatory Body (Statutory, Chartered, Incorporated)
Institute of Chartered Accountants in England and Wales

Nature of Register (Statutory or voluntary, title or function, licence to practice etc.)
N/A

Number Registered
104,559

Professional Institution/Association (if different from Regulatory Body)
N/A

CPD Policy (Requirement – days/year, accepted activities, mandatory, obligatory or voluntary, current position or target, etc.)

Continuing Professional Education (CPE) is not compulsory for all members, but there are specific groups for whom meeting the requirements of the guidelines is mandatory. The Institute does hope, however, that all its members will demonstrate a commitment to CPE. It is recommended that members achieve

150 CPE points year on year. A member earns one CPE point for every hour of 'unstructured' CPE, and three CPE points for every hour of 'structured' CPE. Unstructured CPE will normally be achieved through private reading and study. Structured CPE is achieved through interaction with other individuals, eg, courses, technical meetings, lectures. Further examples are contained in the guidelines. It is recommended that a member achieves at least 40 per cent of their CPE through structured activities.

CPD Record (Voluntary or compulsory, verification, assessment/certification, credit accumulation, etc.)
Members for whom CPE is compulsory must maintain annual records of their CPE achievement. Members who undertake CPE, even though it is not compulsory for them, will still be expected to record their CPE activities on an annual basis. It is for the individual member to decide what is relevant and constitutes CPE in relation to their own work. Members are not expected to submit their CPE records unless specifically requested to do so by the Institute. The recording of CPE involves maintaining details of reading and research, including titles of publications and subject areas covered, title and organizers of course/lectures attended, details of additional qualifications studied for. The appropriate number of CPE points should be awarded.

Enforcement/Monitoring
Very generally, a member is required to undertake CPE in cases where he or she is working towards an additional 'qualification' such as entitlement to hold a Practising Certificate, or advancement to Fellowship. At the time of application the member's CPE details may be scrutinized. The JMU will monitor whether or not a firm has appropriate CPE programmes in place for the compulsory categories of audit and investment business.

Sanctions
There are no sanctions against members who do not comply with the guidelines, although the Institute may not grant a specific application if CPE compliance is a requirement and cannot be demonstrated by the member.

CPD Providers (Courses, distance learning, etc.)
Accountancy Business Group, the Institute's Library, Accountancy TV, District Societies, firms or companies and independent providers.

Guidance to Providers
No specific guidance. It is for our members to decide if a particular activity is relevant and useful CPE for their purposes. If they consider it is, they may award themselves the appropriate number of CPE points. We believe our members are best placed to make this decision.

Accreditation of Courses (Policy, practice, funding, etc.)
The Institute does not accredit CPE courses.

Funding (Subscription, sponsorship, grant in aid, etc.)
None.

Facilitators (Assistance to Registrants, CPD Managers, Postgraduate Deans, etc.)
Post-qualification Section will offer advice to members on CPE.

CPD Information to Registrants
CPE guidelines issued to all members (excluding retired members) on an annual basis.

Profession: **Actuaries**

Regulatory Body (Statutory, Chartered, Incorporated)
Institute of Actuaries and Faculty of Actuaries

Nature of Register (Statutory or voluntary, title or function, licence to practice, etc.)
Actuaries can practise by gaining the qualification FIA or FFA. However, there are particular requirements of the DTI for those wishing to be Appointed Actuaries of life insurance companies and Friendly Societies, and of SIB for those wishing to be authorized to give investment advice.

Number Registered

No. of Fellows	Institute		Faculty	
	Home	3,059	Home	615
	Overseas	958	Overseas	229

Professional Institution/Association (if different from Regulatory Body)
N/A

CPD Policy (Requirement – days/year, accepted activities, mandatory, obligatory or voluntary, current position or target, etc.)
Formal activity 15 hours per year. Attendance at meetings and courses. In-house events can count for up to 7.5 hours each year. Informal activity 52 hours per year. Reading and other individual activities.

CPD Record (Voluntary or compulsory, verification, assessment/certification, credit accumulation, etc.)
The keeping of a CPD record is voluntary except for those for whom CPD is mandatory.

Enforcement/Monitoring
For most actuaries the undertaking of CPD is an ethical responsibility. For actuaries required to undertake CPD for a practising certificate as an Appointed Actuary or for authorization to give investment advice, an annual self-certification is required by the Institute. Attendance of newly qualified actuaries on professionalism courses is monitored.

Sanctions
Actuaries failing to meet the CPD requirements for Appointed Actuary or authorization for investment advice would not be included on the Institute's list of actuaries in these categories.

CPD Providers (Courses, distance learning, etc.)
The professional bodies themselves (Institute and Faculty) are the main providers. Actuaries can attend events of other providers if they consider them to be relevant.

Guidance to Providers
None.

Accreditation of Courses (Policy, practice, funding, etc.)
There is a policy not to accredit events.

Funding (Subscription, sponsorship, grant in aid, etc.)
None. Employers pay costs of events for individuals. Some events are provided free of charge through the professional body, eg, sessional meetings where papers are read.

Facilitators (Assistance to registrants, CPD managers, Postgraduate Deans, etc.)
The Chief Education Executive has responsibility for the development of CPD opportunities.

CPD Information to Registrants
Information is contained in the members' handbook of the profession.

Profession: **Architecture**

Regulatory Body (Statutory, Chartered, Incorporated)
ARCUK

Nature of Register (Statutory or voluntary, title or function, licence to practice, etc.)
Statutory

Number Registered
31,000

Professional Institution/Association (if different from Regulatory Body)
Royal Institute of British Architects

CPD Policy (Requirement – days/years, accepted activities, mandatory, obligatory or voluntary, current position or target, etc.)
Since 1 January 1993, CPD has been obligatory and a duty of membership of RIBA. Byelaw re CPD scheme accepted and agreed by Privy Council in Spring 1993. Members are required to undertake a minimum of 35 hours a year of CPD or to spread the hours over three years – 105 hours to be averaged out according to their particular needs and circumstances. RIBA believes that any personal development which can be clearly seen in the context of professional needs is acceptable to CPD. The Institute recommends a *further* 35 hrs per annum of CPD (making a total of 70 hours per annum) for every member throughout their working life.

CPD Record (Voluntary or compulsory, verification, assessment/certification, credit accumulation, etc.)
Members are provided with a personal development plan and record sheet for their use. Members complete the plan voluntarily.

Enforcement/monitoring
CPD is regarded as an architect's duty. RIBA does not monitor compliance with this at this time.

Sanctions
CPD is a duty of membership as a result of the passing of a byelaw.

CPD Providers (Courses, distance learning, etc.)
RIBA has produced a series of open learning packages called the RIBA Professional Studies in British Architectural Practice, of which there are currently 75 titles. RIBA centrally supports its facilitators in the provision of regional CPD opportunities, and arranges events at branch, region and headquarters levels. RIBA CPD/Open Learning Video Library produces (with industry help) videos suitable for CPD.

Guidance to providers
RIBA and the BMP produced a guide for building materials producers, suppliers and trade associations providing CPD. Providers Forum in formation: intended to include companies/institutions/practices.

Accreditation of Courses (Policy, practice, funding, etc.)
RIBA does not at present accredit or validate courses or learning opportunities on the grounds of credibility and practicality; under review.

Funding (Subscription, sponsorship, grant in aid, etc.)
Facilitators are funded by grant-aid provided from the subscriptions of RIBA members. Sponsorship has been received in the past for particular projects and will be sought for future initiatives. Regional subscription scheme, tickets at-the-door.

Facilitators (Assistance to Registrants, CPD Managers, Postgraduate Deans, etc.)
Each of the 11 RIBA regions as well as the RIAS, RSUA and Society of Architects in Wales has a paid CPD manager and a voluntary CPD convenor. RIBA Head Office has a CPD liaison officer, supported by education department staff.

CPD Information to Registrants
All members receive a guide to CPD and a personal development plan and are made aware that CPD is a duty of membership. An article on CPD is always in RIBA's monthly journal and CPD usually features in the regional newsletters. CPD convenors normally attend regional education committees/practice committees/councils and disseminate CPD information.

Profession: **Chemical Engineering**

Regulatory body (Statutory, Chartered, Incorporated)
The Institution of Chemical Engineers

Nature of Register (Statutory or voluntary, title or function, licence to practice etc.)
Voluntary Register to title and Chartered Chemical Engineer.

Number Registered
8,619

Professional Institution/Association (if different from Regulatory Body)
N/A

CPD Policy (Requirement – days/year, accepted activities, mandatory, obligatory or voluntary, current position or target, etc.)
Under review: IChemE is committed to helping its members to plan and undertake an on-going CPD programme. Evaluation of a formal policy is under way.

CPD Record (Voluntary or compulsory, verification, assessment/certification, credit accumulation, etc.)
Awaiting outcome of policy review: currently voluntary.

The policy review will recommend assistance from the IChemE to members in planning their CPD.

Enforcement/Monitoring
Awaiting outcome of policy review. Likely outcome: IChemE will monitor log books, leaving monitoring to the individual practitioners.

Sanctions
Awaiting outcome of policy review. Likely outcome: sanctions will not be applied.

CPD Providers (Courses, distance learning, etc.)
The IChemE runs short courses for members in the process field.

Modular MSc in process safety and loss prevention in association with HSE and University of Sheffield.

Video and slide training packages in safety, loss prevention and environmental protection.

Programme of conferences and seminars.

IChemE (together with ICE, IMechE, IEE) sponsors a diploma in engineering management.

Guidance to providers
None

Accreditation of Courses (Policy, practice, funding, etc.)
None.

Funding (Subscription, sponsorship, grant in aid, etc.)
Open access to Institution courses and learned society activities;
otherwise participants or their employers pay course fees as charged.

Facilitators (Assistance to Registrants, CPD Managers, Postgraduate Deans, etc.)
CPD information is available from the Institution.

CPD Information to Registrants
Institution publishes programmes of meetings and courses.

Profession: **Civil Engineering**

Regulatory Body (Statutory, Chartered, Incorporated)
The Institution of Civil Engineers

Nature of Register (Statutory or voluntary, title or function, licence to practice, etc.)
Voluntary register of title – Chartered Civil Engineer

Number Registered
48,185

Professional Institution/Association (if different from Regulatory Body)
N/A

CPD Policy (Requirement – days/year, accepted activities, mandatory, obligatory or voluntary, current position or target, etc.)
Five days per year obligatory/expected to satisfy requirements of rules for professional conduct.

Accepted activities: courses, seminars and technical meetings; conferences, committees and working parties in a managerial capacity; private studies of a structured nature; correspondence courses, Open University courses and other supervised study packages; research and post-qualification studies; technical authorship or preparation of lectures for an organized event.

CPD Record (Voluntary or compulsory, verification, assessment/certification, credit accumulation, etc.)
Members provided with a record of continuing professional development (ICE 108), an A5 booklet to record lifetime CPD on a voluntary basis: no verification or certification: record required to support application to grade of Fellow.

Enforcement/Monitoring
None.

Sanctions
None. Lack of CPD would be a breach of rules for professional conduct which would be taken into account in any investigation of non-professional behaviour.

CPD Providers (Courses, distance learning, etc.)
The Institution (learned society activities), universities, colleges and commercial course providers including CTA Services Ltd. The ICE (together with IMechE, IEE and IChemE) sponsors the Diploma in Engineering Management (DipEM)

Guidance to Providers
None

Accreditation of Courses (Policy, practice, funding, etc.)
None; it is left to the individual and his/her employer to decide the value of each course.

Funding (Subscription, sponsorship, grant in aid, etc.)
Learned society activities by Institution is a service to members covered by subscription; otherwise participants or their employers pay course fees as charged.

Facilitators (Assistance to Registrants, CPD Managers, Postgraduate Deans, etc.)
CPD information is available from the Institution in London. Local associations advise on local opportunities for CPD. The ICE publishes 'Management Development in the Construction Industry–Guidelines for the Professional Engineer' – a personal development plan for the civil engineer in management.

CPD Information to Registrants
Courses guide for the Construction Industry (ICE 105) published in Jan, May and September. Courses categorized as technical studies (TS) or professional/management studies (CS) listed by local association area, overseas and distance learning.

Profession: **Dentistry**

Regulatory Body (Statutory, Chartered, Incorporated)
Statutory.

Nature of Register (Statutory or voluntary, title or function, licence to practice, etc.)
Statutory, protected title, licence to practise.

Number Registered
27,068 at 1 January 1993.

Professional Institution/Association (if different from Regulatory Body)
British Dental Association

CPD Policy (Requirement – days/year, accepted activities, mandatory, obligatory or voluntary, current position or target, etc.)
There is a general requirement within the GDC's notes of guidance on fitness to practise that dentists should keep their professional knowledge up-to-date.

The NHS puts a similar requirement upon dentists in NHS general practice. There is no defined minimum commitment to continuing professional education, either in the private or NHS sectors. The GDC has just issued a major consultation document on a strategy for dental education at all levels, so continuing professional development is very much a current issue.

CPD Record (Voluntary or compulsory, verification, assessment/certification, credit accumulation etc.)
There is no compulsory record of CPD, with the exception of a record book for new graduates, and some other new entrants, during a mandatory year of vocation training before unsupervised practice in NHS general dental services. A record is kept by some practitioners on attendance at some courses which qualify for certain fees; in general terms there is a record of the number of practitioners attending NHS-provided postgraduate courses, and of the uptake of NHS-funded peer review projects.

Enforcement/monitoring
There is no enforcement or monitoring of CPD regarding the mandatory vocational training scheme.

Sanctions
There are no sanctions directly related to CPD.

CPD Providers (Courses, distance learning, etc.)
CPD providers include the NHS through its regional structure of postgraduate dental deans and postgraduate tutors, and the Department of Health directly. Facilities include hands-on courses and lectures at postgraduate centres, and distance learning packages including videos and self-assessment manuals/packages. Work is currently being done on computer-assisted learning opportunities. Other providers include the private sector, laboratories and membership organizations such as BDA through its branches, sections and groups, the relevant faculties of the Royal Colleges of Surgeons and specialist interest groups such as the British Society for Restorative Dentistry. The BDA holds a major annual conference which includes international lectures, hands-on courses and table clinics.

Guidance to providers
For the NHS in England and Wales, priorities for CPD in the general and community dental services are established by the Chief Dental Officer's Committee on Continuing Education and Training (COCET). The profession is very well represented on COCET.

Accreditation of Courses (policy, practice, funding, etc.)
Courses are accredited, for NHS funding-related purposes mainly, by postgraduate dental deans/directors of postgraduate dental education. Some funding is available in respect of private-sector courses, so these can be covered also, to a limited extent.

Funding (Subscription, sponsorship, grant in aid, etc.)
The major provider of CPD is the NHS, through so-called section 63

arrangements in England and Wales. Courses are provided under S.63 and are free to participants, and travel and subsistence costs may be claimed. All S.63 courses, and other courses approved by deans, qualify for the post-graduate education allowance, currently £92 per half-day, but funding is limited to two claims per practitioner per financial year (ie £184). To qualify for NHS seniority payments, up to ten sessions of approved CPD may be required. In addition, participants may choose to meet course costs directly, or their subscriptions to membership bodies may defray the cost of courses provided by those bodies. Commercial sponsorship from laboratories, supply houses and others is often available.

Facilitators (Assistance to Registrants, CPD Managers, Postgraduate Deans, etc.)
Facilities include the BDA, regional postgraduate offices, regional advisers in vocational training, the faculties of the Royal Colleges of Surgeons, and the National Advice Centre at the RCS, London.

CPD Information to Registrants
Information is provided by the above.

Profession: **Electrical Engineering**

Regulatory Body (Statutory, Chartered, Incorporated)
The Institution of Electrical Engineers

Nature of Register (Statutory or voluntary, title or function, licence to practice, etc.)
Voluntary register of title Chartered Electrical Engineer.

Number Registered
52,817

Professional Institution/Association (if different from Regulatory Body)
N/A

CPD Policy (Requirement – days/year, accepted activities, mandatory, obligatory or voluntary, current position or target, etc.)
Rules of conduct place a specifc responsibility on individual members to maintain and develop professional competence by attention to new developments in science and technology. The Institution believes CPD is an indispensable part of individual professional development and encourages structured programmes of CPD.

CPD Record (Voluntary or compulsory, verification, assessment/certification, credit accumulation, etc.)
Professional Development Record (PDR) binder available to members. Voluntary record of professional and personal development. No verification.

Enforcement/Monitoring
None.

Sanctions
None. Lack of CPD could be breach of the rules of conduct.

CPD Providers (Courses, distance learning, etc.)
Institution organizes short courses for technical updating and management skills. Continuing education modular scheme comprising periods of study, examinations and project work. Over 50 distance learning packages, technical and management subjects. Seminars, colloquia and meetings in London and regions. IEE (together with ICE, IMechE, IChemE) sponsor the diploma in engineering management.

Guidance to Providers
None.

Accreditation of Courses (Policy, practice, funding, etc.)
Approval system for external CPD providers under consideration.

Funding (Subscription, sponsorship, grant in aid, etc.)
Learned society activities by Institution covered by subscription; otherwise participants or their employers pay course fees as charged.

Facilitators (Assistance to Registrants, CPD Managers, Postgraduate Deans, etc.)
Institution provides career advice through telephone 'career helpline'.

CPD Information to Registrants
Professional brief on career development available to members (free). Professional brief on CPD to be developed. Members can seek advice on redundancy, career advice, etc., from a 'Career helpline' telephone enquiry point. This service is confidential and free.

Profession: **Insurance and Financial Services**

Regulatory Body (Statutory, Chartered, Incorporated)
Chartered Insurance Institute

Nature of Register (Statutory or voluntary, title or function, licence to practice, etc.)
Chartered Insurance Practitioners and Chartered Insurers.

Number Registered
Approx. 8,000

Professional Institution/Association (if different from Regulatory Body)
N/A

CPD Policy (Requirement – days/year, accepted activities, mandatory, obligatory or voluntary, current position or target, etc.)
180 points over 3 years, min. 50 points p.a., 3 points for structured; 1 point for unstructured; 2 points for institute work. Mandatory for 'chartered' status.

CPD Record (Voluntary or compulsory, verification, assessment/certification, credit accumulation, etc.)
Self-certification, with a random 5 per cent check p.a.

Enforcement/Monitoring
Random checks only.

Sanctions
Removal of chartered title.

CPD Providers (Courses, distance learning, etc.)
Management trainers, technical trainers, local insurance institutes and employers.

Guidance to providers
Not yet reproduced – CPD will begin 1 January 1995.

Accreditation of Courses (Policy, practice, funding, etc.)
Accreditation of training organizations only.

Funding (Subscription, sponsorship, grant in aid, etc.)
Training will be funded by the industry.

Facilitators (Assistance to Registrants, CPD Managers, Postgraduate Deans, etc.)
Infrastructure not yet in place.

CPD Information to Registrants
Not yet produced.

Profession: **The Law; Solicitors**

Regulatory Body (Statutory, Chartered, Incorporated)
The Law Society for England and Wales

Nature of Register (Statutory or voluntary, title or function, licence to practice, etc.)
Statutory obligation for solicitors' names to appear on the register maintained by the Law Society.

Number Registered
75,000 including those retired; 57,000 holding Practising Certificates

Professional Institution/Association (if different from Regulatory Body)
N/A

CPD Policy (Requirement – days/year, accepted activities, mandatory, obligatory or voluntary, current position or target, etc.)
Mandatory. Solicitors who work in a legal capacity are required to undertake CPD whether or not they hold a Practising Certificate. The CPD year runs from 1 November to the following 31 October. For newly admitted solicitors,

1 hour per month from their date of admission to the following 1 November. First year, 16 hours CPD and a Professional Development Course; second year, 16 hours CPD; third year, 16 hours CPD and a Best Practice Course; from the fourth year onwards, 48 hours every 3 years.

CPD Record (Voluntary or compulsory, verification, assessment/certification, credit accumulation, etc.)
Training record supplied by the Society.

Enforcement/monitoring
Training record can be requested by the Law Society at any time. Failure to keep up-to-date with developments in law and practice impairs the proper standard of work, contrary to Practice Rule 1.

Sanctions
The Practising Certificate requires a compulsory declaration on the amount of CPD taken over the previous year. Persistent non-compliers may have their Practising Certificate delayed or removed, in extreme circumstances. This is extremely rare. More often, information and help from the Law Society will correct any non-compliance.

CPD Providers (Courses, distance learning, etc.)
Various. Higher education, private providers.

Guidance to Providers
The Law Society authorizes course providers according to a set of strict criteria: the provider must be of good quality; the courses must be relevant to solicitors; speakers must have experience in the subject area; and materials must be provided for any courses lasting more than an hour. A Law Society brochure sets out these criteria, after which the provider may apply for accreditation.

Accreditation of Courses (policy, practice, funding, etc.)
See 'Guidance to Providers'.

Funding
The onus is on the individual solicitor to comply with the requirements. Employers are not obliged to fund CPD, although many do so.

Facilitators (Assistance to Registrants, CPD Managers, Postgraduate deans, etc.)
Local Law Societies, acting independently from the Law Society, may have education committees. Four regional offices (including one in Brussels) provide information. A conference for the honorary secretaries of the local Law Societies ensures that they are themselves up-to-date.

CPD Information to Registrants
Guidelines are sent to every newly admitted solicitor explaining the system. Information including a register of course providers is sent to all firms and is available from the Society on request. Information is also included in the

'Gazette', local higher education institutions and other course providers also advertise.

Profession: **Marine Engineering**

Regulatory Body (Statutory, Chartered, Incorporated)
The Institute of Marine Engineers

Nature of Register (statutory or voluntary, title or function, licence to practice, etc.)
Voluntary register of title Chartered Marine Engineer.

Number Registered
10,430

Professional Institution/Association (if different from Regulatory Body)
N/A.

CPD Policy (Requirement – days/year, accepted activities, mandatory, obligatory or voluntary, current position or target, etc.)

IMarE is committed to a CPD programme that will encourage a joint commitment by members and their employers to personal CPD, thereby ensuring that members maintain a degree of professional competence appropriate to their professional standing. Voluntary; no minimum requirement.

CPD Record (Voluntary or compulsory, verification, assessment/certification, credit accumulation, etc.)
Institute to publish a career log book. Members encouraged to keep record. Voluntary; no verification.

Enforcement/monitoring
None.

Sanctions
None.

CPD Providers (Courses, distance learning, etc.)
Institute to hold a series of one day seminars/workshops.

Conferences, seminars and technical meetings, organized by Institute in London and regions.

Guidance to providers
None.

Accreditation of Courses (Policy, practice, funding, etc.)
None.

Funding (Subscription, sponsorship, grant in aid, etc.)
Learned society activities by Institute a service to members covered by subscription; otherwise participants or their employers pay course fees charged.

Facilitators (Assistance to Registrants, CPD Managers, Postgraduate Deans, etc.)
None.

CPD Information to Registrants
Institute to produce a leaflet 'Continuing Professional Development – Career Development Programme'.

Profession: **Mechanical Engineering**

Regulatory Body (Statutory, Chartered, Incorporated)
The Institution of Mechanical Engineers

Nature of Register (Statutory or voluntary, title or function, licence to practice, etc.)
Voluntary register of title Chartered Mechanical Engineer.

Number Registered
46,632

Professional Institution/Association (if different from Regulatory Body)
N/A.

CPD Policy (Requirement – days/year, accepted activities, mandatory, obligatory or voluntary, current position or target, etc.)
Professionally active members are expected to undertake a minimum of 50 hours per year on CPD related subjects. CPD is not mandatory at the present time.

CPD Record (Voluntary or compulsory, verification, assessment/certification, credit accumulation, etc.)
Professional development record available to members. Voluntary; no verification. 'Continuing Professional Development – A Guide for Mechanical Engineers', is available free of charge to members.

Enforcement/Monitoring
None.

Sanctions
None.

CPD Providers (Courses, distance learning, etc.)
Technical divisions and special interest groups organize conferences, seminars and technical lectures (also accessible to non-members). IMechE co-sponsor the diploma in engineering management.

Guidance to Providers
None.

Accreditation of Courses (Policy, practice, funding, etc.)
None.

Funding (Subscription, sponsorhip, grant in aid, etc.)
Learned society activities by the Institution is a service to members covered by subscription; otherwise participants or their employer pay course fees charged.

Facilitators (Assistance to Registrants, CPD Managers, Postgraduate Deans, etc.)
None.

CPD Information to Registrants
Short course information available on ECCTIS/PICKUP database through information library service

Profession: **Medicine**

Regulatory body (Statutory, Chartered, Incorporated)
General Medical Council has statutory responsibility for pre-registration period, Royal Colleges for post-registration period.

Nature of Register (Statutory or voluntary, title or function, licence to practice, etc.)
Statutory obligation for doctors' names to appear on the medical register before they may practice.

Number Registered
187,696 at 9 April 1994.

Professional Institution/Association (if different from Statutory Body)
British Medical Association

CPD Policy (Requirement – days/year, accepted activities, mandatory, obligatory or voluntary, current position or target, etc.)
Varies from speciality to speciality. NHS reforms have introduced a requirement to participate in clinical audit. Other activities are voluntary. General practice is the most organized system so far, through the Postgraduate Education Allowance (PGEA) scheme which allows GPs access to part of their income, only after proof of participation in continuing medical education.

CPD Record (Voluntary or compulsory, verification, assessment/certification, credit accumulation, etc.)
See 'CPD Policy' – essentially voluntary.

Enforcement/monitoring
Appropriate Royal College supervises continuing medical education. Continuing professional development in areas such as management education; interprofessional relations are still in developmental stage.

Sanctions
1. GPs lose about 5 per cent of income. 2. No access to career grade posts without accreditation.

CPD Providers (Courses, distance learning etc.)
Various – courses, workshops, distance learning packages, etc. provided by many organizations including the Royal Colleges, the BMA, drug companies, private companies, etc.

Guidance to providers
Via the Royal Colleges.

Accreditation of Courses (Policy, practice, funding, etc.)
Via postgraduate deans, college tutors, and regional GP clinical advisers.

Funding (Subscription, sponsorship, grant in aid, etc.)
Depends on provider – delegates' fees, sponsorship, etc.

Facilitators (Assistance to Registrants, CPD Managers, Postgraduate Deans, etc.)
See 'Accreditation of Courses'.

CPD Information to Registrants
Via Royal Colleges and regional postgraduate deans.

CPD Contact
Royal Colleges (Joint Higher Training Committees), British Medical Association (Secretary of Medical Education Working Party), local college tutors.

Profession: **Mining Engineering**

Regulatory Body (Statutory, Chartered, Incorporated)
The Institution of Mining Engineers

Nature of Register (Statutory or voluntary, title or function, licence to practice, etc.)
Voluntary register of title Chartered Mining Engineer.

Number Registered
1,910

Professional Institution/Association (if different from Regulatory Body)
N/A.

CPD Policy (Requirement – days/year, accepted activities, mandatory, obligatory or voluntary, current position or target, etc.)
Institution encourages members to enhance their knowledge and skills through planned CPD. Voluntary: no minimum requirement.

CPD Record (Voluntary or compulsory, verification, assessment/certification, credit accumulation, etc.)
Use of Engineering Council 'Career Manager' recommended, voluntary: no verification.

Enforcement/Monitoring
None.

Sanctions
None.

CPD Providers (Courses, distance learning, etc.)
Institution organizes conferences, symposia and technical meetings nationally and through UK branches.

Guidance to providers
None.

Accreditation of Courses (Policy, practice, funding, etc.)
None.

Funding (Subscription, sponsorship, grant in aid, etc.)
Learned society activities by Institution a service to members and covered by subscription; otherwise participants or their employers pay course fees charged.

Facilitators (Assistance to Registrants, CPD Managers, Postgraduate Deans, etc.)
Individual advice is available to members through the Institution's headquarters staff.

CPD Information to Registrants
None published.

Profession: **Optometry**

Regulatory Body (Statutory, Chartered, Incorporated)
General Optical Council

Nature of Register (Statutory or voluntary, title or function, licence to practice, etc.)
Statutory licence to practice.

Number Registered
Approx 6,800

Professional Institution/Association (if different from Regulatory Body)
British College of Optometrists is the public benefit and examining body; 95 per cent of optometrists are members.

CPD Policy (Requirement – days/year, accepted activities, mandatory, obligatory or voluntary, current position or target, etc.)
Mandatory for supervisors of pre-registration students. Moves to make CPD mandatory for examiners and, in the longer-term, for all members of profession. Course attendance or lecturing on courses is the normal fulfilment of requirement.

CPD Record (Voluntary or compulsory, verification, assessment/certification, credit accumulation, etc.)
Self-regulating and satisfied by statement of courses attended/lectures given. Little or no verification.

Enforcement/Monitoring
Annual monitoring of self-regulating forms

Sanctions
Removal as supervisor.

CPD Providers (Courses, distance learning, etc.)
Local and national courses. Distance learning package. Higher diplomas.

Guidance to Providers
None

Accreditation of Courses (Policy, practice, funding, etc.)
None

Funding (Subscription, sponsorship, grant in aid, etc.)
Some courses are funded by government monies, the vast majority are not. Funding provides for distance learning package, quarterly audiocassettes, about two videos per year; funding from government and occasionally sponsorship.

Facilitators (Assistance to Registrants, CPD Managers, Postgraduate Deans, etc.)
In due course this role will be assumed by the College's academic department.

CPD Information to Registrants
Not often called for from the College as courses are run mostly at local society level.

Profession: **Patent Agent**

Regulatory Body (Statutory, Chartered, Incorporated)
Chartered Institute of Patent Agents

Nature of Register (Statutory or voluntary, title or function, licence to practice, etc.)
Statutory. Registered Patent Agents must become Fellows of the Institute to use the title Chartered Patent Agent.

Number Registered
1282

Professional Institution/Association (if different from Regulatory Body)
N/A.

CPD Policy (Requirement – days/year, accepted activities, mandatory, obligatory or voluntary, current position or target, etc.)
To maintain name on register, no requirement to update. For membership of the Institute, no specific requirement but a guideline on the observance of the rules of conduct states: 'Members are expected to keep their relevant knowledge and expertise up-to-date to the best of their ability'.

CPD Record (Voluntary or compulsory, verification, assessment/certification, credit accumulation, etc.)
No checks are made to confirm whether CPD has been undertaken. No records of CPD activity are required.

Enforcement/monitoring
None.

Sanctions
In a disciplinary case, the Institute could exclude a member or suspend him or her for up to two years for breach of the rules of professional conduct. The Secretary of State could order erasure from the register if he or she concluded that an agent's conduct was discreditable.

CPD Providers (Courses, distance learning, etc.)
The Institute itself organizes courses and conferences for its members, though not to a great extent.

Queen Mary and Westfield College has chair of Intellectual Property Law and provides some courses.

Guidance to providers
None prepared.

Accreditation of Courses (Policy, practice, funding, etc.)
No accreditation.

Funding (Subscription, sponsorship, grant in aid, etc.)
No funding – courses are self-financing through delegates fees.

Facilitators (Assistance to Registrants, CPD Managers, Postgraduate Deans, etc.)
None.

CPD Information to Registrants
None.

Profession: **Pharmacy**

Regulatory Body (Statutory, Chartered, Incorporated)
Statutory

Nature of Register (Statutory or voluntary, title or function, licence to practice etc.)
Statutory, Register of Pharmaceutical Chemists. Licence to Practice.

Number Registered
39,443

Professional Institution/Association (if different from Regulatory Body)
Royal Pharmaceutical Society of Great Britain

CPD Policy (Requirement – day, year, accepted activities, mandatory, obligatory or voluntary, current position or target, etc.)
Voluntary annual target for participation in Continuing Education (CE) of 30 hours per year, within which pharmacists are encourage to meet with other pharmacists on at least one occasion. Professional obligation to continually review and update knowledge to provide a competent service exists under code of ethics.

CPD Record (Voluntary or compulsory, verficiation, assessment/certification, credit accumulation, etc.)
Voluntary – the RPSGB has recently provided a continuing professional development planner and record to every registered pharmacist in Great Britain. Tutors of pre-registration trainees are required to provide evidence of participation in 15 hours of continuing education activity per year.

Enforcement/monitoring
There is no enforcement. National postgraduate education centres keep computer records of participation for their own purposes, but there is no monitoring at present by the RPSGB.

Sanctions
None.

CPD Providers (Courses, distance learning, etc.)
Major providers are Centre for Pharmacy Postgraduate Education (CPPE) (England), Welsh Centre for Postgraduate Pharmaceutical Education (WCPPE), Scottish Centre for Post-qualification Pharmaceutical Education (SCPPE), College of Pharmacy Practice, RPSGB branches, National Pharmaceutical Association, pharmaceutical companies and NHS regions (hospital pharmacists).

Guidance to Providers
National continuing education syllabus for pharmacy exists to provide guidance to both providers and participating pharmacists. Checklist for postgraduate course providers and users has been produced in relation to formal postgraduate courses. The RPSGB has recently approved a code of practice for providers of continuing education (CE) programmes in pharmacy which has been promoted to providers of CE throughout Great Britain.

Accreditation of Courses (Policy, practice, funding, etc.)
There is no course accreditation at present.

Funding (Subscription, sponsorship, grant in aid, etc.)
The government health departments fund the national centres of postgradu-

ate education for pharmacists, the CPPE, WCPPE and the SCPPE. There is some funding available for hospital pharmacy CE provision through the NHS. Pharmaceutical companies sponsor some courses. Other courses are self-financing.

Facilitators (Assistance to Registrants, CPD Managers, Postgraduate Deans, etc.)
The CPPE employs 70 tutors to facilitate provision at local level. The WCPPE employs three full-time learning facilitators covering North, Mid and South West, and South East Wales. The SCPPE employs 11 local tutors, a national postgraduate tutor and three specialist postgraduate tutors.

CPD Information to Registrants
Guidance on Continuing Professional Development is issued to all pharmacists biannually via a medicines, ethics and practice guide. The CPPE produces a quarterly catalogue of CE events which is mailed to every pharmacist in England. Similar arrangements exist in Wales and Scotland with additional publicity via *The Pharmaceutical Journal*. Programmes of RPSGB local branch meetings are mailed to pharmacists periodically and again these are supplemented by publicity in *The Pharmaceutical Journal*.

Profession: **Psychology**

Regulatory Body (Statutory, Chartered, Incorporated)
The British Psychological Society incorporated by Royal Charter

Nature of Register (Statutory or voluntary, title or function, licence to practice, etc.)
Register of Chartered Psychologists in which the title is protected on a voluntary basis.

Number Registered
7,278

Professional Institution/Association (if different from Regulatory Body)
N/A.

CPD Policy (Requirement – days/year, accepted activities, mandatory, obligatory or voluntary, current position or target, etc.)
The Society's code of conduct requires psychologists to 'endeavour to maintain and develop their professional competence to recognise and work within its limits and to identify and ameliorate factors which restrict it'. This places an obligation on chartered psychologists to engage in some form of continuing of professional development on an essentially voluntary basis. The Society has a standing committee for the coordination of continuing professional development. Psychologists will become increasingly aware of their need for CPD. Surveys of what is actually carried out will be undertaken and eventually formal expectations will be set, so that renewal of the practising certificate might become possible only if there is evidence of CPD having been completed.

CPD Record (Voluntary or compulsory, verification, assessment/certification, credit accumulation, etc.)
The Society has no formal procedure whereby members maintain a CPD record. One of its professional divisions, the division of educational child psychology, has developed a log book which members of the division are encouraged to complete on an annual basis.

Enforcement/Monitoring
The Society has no formal basis for monitoring or enforcing CPD

Sanctions
If a complaint is received about a member and, following investigation, a disciplinary committee came to the conclusion that professional misconduct had been found as a result of a member failing to maintain their professional competence, all the sanctions open to the disciplinary committee could be drawn on, including ultimately the final sanction of removal from the Register of Chartered Psychologists.

CPD Providers (Courses, distance learning, etc.)
CPD is provided by university institutions, privately-run courses, year-long formal postgraduate qualifications and shorter courses. Many of the conferences and scientific meetings put on each year by the Society are relevant for the purposes of CPD. However, the Society's definition includes opportunities for individual psychologists to read the relevant literature and even engage in personal study, keeping themselves up-to-date with developments in the profession.

Guidance to Providers
Guidance to providers is largely in the form of criteria for the accreditation of courses as listed in the next section.

Accreditation of Courses (policy, practice, funding, etc.)
The Society has published criteria for the recognition of short courses and the accreditation of longer courses. Recommended courses are entitled to use a symbol indicating that they are approved by the Society.

Funding (Subscription, sponsorship, grant in aid, etc.)
The majority of psychologists work for publicly-funded organizations such as local authorities, the National Health Service, the Prison Service, or the Civil Service. To a large measure they are dependent on funding from employers. Those in private practice inevitably have to fund their own continuing professional development and indeed many in the public sector will attend conferences, meeting the expenses from their own pocket. It is the lack of funding that leads to the difficulties in making continuing professional development mandatory.

Facilitators (Assistance to Registrants, CPD Managers, Postgraduate Deans, etc.)
The main professional divisions of the Society have training committees or

equivalent volunteer-run committees which promote continuing professional development. Some administrative support is available to these committees from the staff of the Society, but there are no formal CPD managers or postgraduate deans, etc. Representatives of the various division training committees all serve on the standing committee for the coordination of the continuing professional development of psychologists, which is represented on the Society's membership and qualifications board.

CPD Information to Registrants
The Society has a house organ *The Psychologist* which carries advertisements for courses and conferences.

Profession: **Physiotherapy**

Regulatory Body (Statutory, Chartered, Incorporated)
Council for the Professions Supplementary to Medicine (Statutory); Chartered Society of Physiotherapy (Chartered)

Nature of Register (Statutory or voluntary, title or function, licence to practice, etc.)
Statutory obligation for physiotherapists' names to appear on the register maintained by the Council before they may practice in the NHS. Otherwise, voluntary registration; title of physiotherapist is not yet protected.

Number Registered
25,000 (total membership of CSP): 21,000 (fully paid-up/practising members of CSP)

Professional Institution/Association (if different from Regulatory Body)
Chartered Society of Physiotherapy

CPD Policy (Requirement – days/year, accepted activities, mandatory, obligatory or voluntary, current position or target, etc.)
No mandatory system, but CPD is encouraged. Currently CPD policy is being developed to broaden base of post-registration education. Already in place is the Physiotherapy Access to Continuing Education (PACE) scheme, a practice-based system of continuing education which contributes to professional development through a credit-rating system. PACE promotes flexible continuing education opportunities; encourages physiotherapists to take responsibility for their own learning; and includes words that confer academic and professional recognition. A CPD policy will be published in Winter 1994.

CPD Record (Voluntary or compulsory, verification, assessment/certification, credit accumulation, etc.)
No compulsory record, but a professional development diary is available to all members and will be distributed to student members in the academic year 1994/5.

Enforcement/monitoring
No formal system.

Sanctions
Rules of professional conduct.

CPD Providers (Courses, distance learning, etc.)
Various – clinical physiotherapists (particularly through the clinical interest groups); the higher education sector (now that physiotherapy schools have pre-registration courses, they have expanded into post-registration and post-graduate), and employers (through in-service programmes and education).

Guidance to Providers
See 'Accreditation of Courses'.

Accreditation of Courses (Policy, practice, funding, etc.)
The CSP operates a centralized accreditation system in association with the University of Greenwich, through which courses run by the higher education sector may gain credit-rating with academic and professional currency. Courses accredited by most higher education institutions may also gain recognition with PACE.

Funding (Subscription, sponsorship, grant in aid, etc.)
Some physiotherapists may obtain funding from their employers or their hospitals; the Society has a small fund for post-registration and postgraduate study. Many, however, pay for their own CPD. Funding is one of the key issues for physiotherapists.

Facilitators (Assistance to Registrants, CPD Managers, Postgraduate Deans, etc.)
No formal structure; however, there is informal peer-group support, and role of managers, professional body, higher education sector.

CPD Information to Registrants
The PACE catalogue is available to members together with information on wider postgraduate and post-registration opportunities. Shorter courses are advertised each month in the *Physiotherapists* journal. Clinical interest groups also provide information on CPD in their subject areas. To date, nearly 400 courses and modules are recognized within the scheme.

Profession: **Structural Engineering**

Regulatory Body (Statutory, Chartered, Incorporated)
The Institution of Structural Engineers

Nature of Register (Statutory or voluntary, title or function, licence to practice, etc.)
Voluntary Register of Title, Chartered Structural Engineer

Number Registered
9,168

Professional Institution/Association (if different from Regulatory Body)
N/A.

CPD Policy (Requirement – days/year, accepted activities, mandatory, obligatory or voluntary, current position or target, etc.)
The Institution recommends 20 hrs per year involvement in CPD for all members. Currently CPD is not mandatory for members but evidence of active involvement over the past five years is required for Fellowship.

CPD Record (Voluntary or compulsory, verification, assessment/certification, credit accumulation, etc.)
The 'Career Planner and Diary' is available for use by individual members and is available free to all newly elected members.

Enforcement/Monitoring
None.

Sanctions
None.

CPD Providers (Courses, distance learning, etc.)
IStructE CPD programme of courses provides one-day and half-day events on technical, management and law subjects. Videos are available for hire. Evening meetings organized by branches.

Guidance to providers
CPD handbook provides guidance on CPD to branches, members and firms.

Accreditation of Courses (Policy, practice, funding, etc.)
None; responsibility for suitability rests with the individual.

Funding (Subscription, sponsorship, grant in aid, etc.)
Learned society activities by institution a service to members covered by subscription; otherwise participants or their employers pay course fees charged.

Facilitators (Assistance to Registrants, CPD Managers, Postgraduate Deans, etc.)
CPD representatives in branches: regular feedback meeting; CPD questionnaire to solicit feedback on CPD handbook and members' problems.

CPD Information to Registrants

Profession: **Surveying**

Regulatory Body (Statutory, Chartered, Incorporated)
Royal Institution of Chartered Surveyors

Nature of Register (Statutory or voluntary, title or function, licence to practice, etc.)
Statutory; practitioners must become Associate Members of the RICS to practise as a Chartered Surveyor.

Number Registered
90,576

Professional Institution/Association (if different from Regulating Body)
N/A.

CPD Policy (Requirement – days/year, accepted activities, mandatory, obligatory or voluntary, current position or target etc.)
Obligatory; a requirement for membership upgrading. Minimum CPD per year 20 hours (60 hours in three years).

CPD Record (Voluntary or compulsory, verification, assessment/certification, credit accumulation, etc.)
CPD profile (Filofax card).

Enforcement/Monitoring
Random monitoring by sample surveys annually. Those members questioned must produce evidence of compliance. If members are in difficulties, they are counselled and monitored again.

Sanctions
The professional conduct department deals with cases of non-compliance, although it is unlikely that the majority of cases would reach this stage.

CPD Providers (Courses, distance learning, etc.)
Various: local educational establishments, commercial institutions, higher education.

Guidance to Providers
There are some instructions available to providers if they wish.

Accreditation of Courses (Policy, practice, funding, etc.)
No.

Funding (Subscription, sponsorship, grant in aid, etc.)
Self-financed, or paid by the employer.

Facilitators (Assistance to Registrants, CPD Managers, Postgraduate Deans, etc.)
Thirty-two RICS branches operate throughout the country.

CPD Information to Registrants
Branch newsletters and the professional journal, *Chartered Surveying Monthly* provide up-to-date information on courses.

Profession: **Town Planning**

Regulatory Body (Statutory, Chartered, Incorporated)
Royal Town Planning Institute

Nature of Register (Statutory or voluntary, title or function, licence to practice, etc.)
Statutory; practitioners must become members of the Institute to practise as a town planner.

Number Registered
18,000

Professional Institution/Association (if different from Regulatory Body)
N/A.

CPD Policy (Requirement – days/year, accepted activities, mandatory, obliga-tory or voluntary, current position or target, etc.)
Obligatory, a new policy as from June 1992; minimum CPD per year: 50 hours in two years.

CPD Record (Voluntary or compulsory, verification, assessment/certification, credit accumulation, etc.)
CPD personal record sheet.

Enforcement/Monitoring
Random monitoring by sample surveys annually. Those members questioned must produce evidence of compliance. If members are in difficulties, they are counselled and monitored again.

Sanctions
The RTPI is hoping not to act like a policing body and maintains that practi-tioners will see the benefit of CPD and willingly carry out their obligation.

CPD Providers (Courses, distance learning, etc.)
Various: local educational establishments, commercial institutions, higher education. The RTPI's own planning and environment department organizes annual conferences.

Guidance to providers
None, but three short statements may be used by providers to the effect that their courses may be considered as CPD by practitioners.

Accreditation of Courses (Policy, practice, funding, etc.)
None

Funding (Subscription, sponsorship, grant in aid, etc.)
Self-financed, or paid by the employer, usually the local authority.

Facilitators (Assistance to Registrants, CPD Managers, Postgraduate Deans, etc.)
Thirteen RTPI branches operate throughout the country. Each branch has its own CPD coordinator and/or CPD contact. Centrally, the CPD unit provides information.

CPD Information to Registrants
A quarterly diary of branch events is sent to every member. Two profession-al journals provide up-to-date information on courses. A practice advice note is also issued.

Profession: **Veterinary Surgeons**

Regulatory Body (Statutory, Chartered, Incorporated)
Royal College of Veterinary Surgeons. Statutory body in terms of the Veterinary Surgeons Act 1966.

Nature of Register (Statutory or voluntary, title or function, licence to practice, etc.)
The register of Veterinary Surgeons is maintained in statutory terms under the Veterinary Surgeons Act.

Number Registered
Active home members – 9744; overseas members – 1680; retired members – 2796.

Professional Institution/Association (if different form Regulatory Body)
British Veterinary Association

CPD Policy (Requirement – day/year, accepted activities, Mandatory, Obligatory or Voluntary, current position or target, etc.)
Voluntary but made an ethical requirement by the code of professional conduct of the RCVS.

CPD Record (Voluntary or compulsory, verification, assessment/certification, credit accumulation, etc.)
No obligation to maintain such.

Enforcement/Monitoring
Since this is a voluntary matter, enforcement does not arise. Monitoring is carried out only in relation to the profession as a whole and not individually. Surveys at three year intervals (approx.) by IMS.

Sanctions
N/A.

CPD Providers (Courses, distance learning, etc.)
BVA, BVA territorial and non-territorial divisions, industry, Ministry of Agriculture, Fisheries & Food, referral centres, specialist societies and veterinary schools.

Accreditation of courses (Policy, practice, funding, etc.)
Accreditation does not arise while CPD is voluntary. However, members of the profession studying for certificates or diplomas of a specialist nature are *de facto* participating in CPD, and their studies do have to meet RCVS requirements.

Funding (Subscription, sponsorship, grant in aid, etc.)
Funding equally from RCVS and BVA. CPD courses are designed as far as possible to be self-financing through the payment of course fees. National and local sponsorship is also received.

Facilitators (Assistance to Registrants, CPD Managers, Postgraduate Deans, etc.)
Centrally BVA and RCVS provide advice and assistance through the joint CPD

committee; at regional level postgraduate deans act as advisers and facilitators.

CPD Information to Registrants
CPD information is regularly provided to the profession through regional post-graduate deans, *The Veterinary Record* and other media.

SECTION 4: HOPES AND FEARS

Each profession was invited to provide a brief note indicating significant future trends for CPD. Contributions from ten institutes are included.

Institute of Actuaries, Faculty of Actuaries

Impact of NCVO on CPD
Given that there is no consensus on Level 5, it is difficult to see how CPD fits in with professional qualifications if a threshold professional model for CPD is adopted.

Accreditation
Will there be a vast industry in accrediting courses while the real issues of quality control remain untouched?

Quality Control
How can we have a good system ensuring that people undertaking CPD are offered a quality, effective course?

Costs of Courses
What do we do for unemployed members of our professional bodies and those having career breaks in general?

Time
Have members got the time to undertake CPD? Will this worsen as more and more companies look for greater efficiencies in staffing levels, putting increasing pressure on those in employment?

Monitoring
How do we monitor CPD, with more and more regulations making a requirement for this to be done?

Measurement

I believe in the benefits of CPD yet there may be a need to demonstrate the tangible benefits in the future. Hopefully, it will become an accepted and established concept just as initial qualifications have.

British Dental Association

Hopes

CPD is a new phrase for the dental profession but one which seems friendly and user-focused. By comparison, CME/CDE (continuing medical/dental education) have tended to be presented more as something 'they' want to happen, than as something to help 'us' gain career satisfaction.

There is growing interest in continuing education and standards within dentistry, especially in general practice. Institutions to support CPD are in place, including a new academic home for general dental practice (the Faculty of General Dental Practitioners in the Royal College of Surgeons).

There is growing understanding of self-assessment, audit and peer review as educational tools. These 'bottom-up' initiatives help dentists to understand their own work and their educational needs and offer a good foundation for practitioner-centred CPD.

Fears

There is a general concern that those who will benefit most from CPD will be most reluctant to participate, or the most difficult for CPD structures to reach. The value of 'mentoring' and one-to-one coaching between colleagues may be understood but it will be difficult to make it happen across the board.

By being centred on individual needs the organization of CPD will necessarily need one-to-one time, which – one way or another – will be very costly. Funding is unlikely to be available on an adequate scale.

CPD (like audit) must be non-threatening and without any possibility of disciplinary consequences. Separation may be difficult to guarantee in small units.

Ever-increasing service needs will put pressure on any CPD time, especially in the university and NHS salaried sectors. In general dental practice, financial pressures will similarly discourage commitment to CPD.

British Medical Association

Unlike some of the other professions, the medical profession makes some distinctions between continuing medical education (CME) and continuing professional development (CPD). CME – the maintenance of professional competence and personal development by the continuous updating of knowledge and skills – is at present primarily the responsibility of the various medical Royal Colleges for different branches of the profession. The broader area of CPD includes a number of key areas where the medical professions' skill and knowledge can be developed. These include management education, inter- and intraprofessional relations in health care, medical ethics, communication skills and other areas where the BMA has acquired considerable expertise and may be regarded as a leader or a principal source of knowledge in the field.

In common with other professions, CPD (and CME) are topical subjects with much debate and discussion going into their development and structuring. The major hope of the BMA is to participate in the development of a cohesive policy for continuing education from entering medical school to leaving a career in medicine. The BMA as the organization representative of all branches of the medical profession, including students, and with a central medico-political function, has an important role to play in the debate surrounding CME and CPD.

Further, the changing professional environment for doctors in the UK and in Europe challenges many of the assumptions about professional development over the course of a career. The BMA is well placed to pick up on these challenges and it hopes to be central in effecting the organization of CPD.

The medical profession fears that the demands of service commitment in the 'new NHS' might erode a medical education system which has to date been regulated by an independent profession. While outside forces cannot be ignored, doctors are keen to maintain their presence at the forefront of medical education.

Effective CME and CPD demand investment. There are fears that the changing structures for the delivery of health care in the UK and the lower priority given to research and training may deny investment in this vital area.

One area of CME gaining attention is that of the introduction of formal recognition of participation in mandatory CME, such as schemes of reaccreditation and sanctions for those not meeting specific targets. There are fears that this may be an expensive and blunt weapon for CME and that it might be better in general to provide support and encouragement to participate, at least until the value to patient care has been fully evaluated and programmes audited. The approach of different sections of the profession varies: general practitioners are exploring individual practitioner and practice reaccreditation, some of the Royal Colleges are introducing mandatory schemes.

Overall, the medical profession hope that CME and CPD will be effectively used to maintain public confidence in the profession and to assist in the achievement of a high quality health care system.

British Psychological Society

Continuing Professional Development is an integral part of the individual's code of conduct on becoming a Chartered Psychologist.

We *hope* that the introduction of a more formalized system of recording and defining CPD will increase the individual's sense of responsibility and professionalism for updating and extending his/her skills and knowledge.

We *hope* that employers will see CPD as maintaining their investment in professional staff; an assurance that their staff are up-to-date and knowledgeable in those aspects in which they are practising and that the expensive initial investment is not lost.

We *hope* that a review of CPD will become a feature of the annual appraisal system for psychologists.

We *fear* that *obligatory* CPD may not be taken seriously by employers as a funding issue, and that *mandatory* CPD could lead to attendance at an event becoming more important than the nature of the event.

We *hope* that we will reach a solution that will encourage employers to support CPD and also encourage psychologists and their employers to make annually a realistic assessment of their professional need and tailor their CPD activities towards this.

British Veterinary Association

Our fears

Any system of CPD should be able to show that it is effective, ie its goals are being achieved. It is therefore essential that those operating the system should be quite clear what its objectives are. One fear is that too much time is devoted to examining means of provision and monitoring the take-up, and too little time to assessing the fundamental aims of the programme. That is to say, is CPD intended:

(a) *to maintain* the professional competence of the individual at graduate/initial qualification level?
(b) *to raise* the level of professional competence of the individual, so that he or she is ahead of the newly qualified?
(c) *to enable* the professional to acquire advanced and in-depth knowledge in a particular sector of his or her professional field?

Once the professional body is clear as to its CPD objectives, it is faced with monitoring the programme to ensure that those objectives are being achieved. At once one is into such matters as validation of courses, approval of 'providing' groups or institutions, and assessment of individual compliance. If followed through in all its aspects, the bureaucracy involved will be considerable. It may prove impractical or stifling to attempt this.

Whether an attempt *is* made to provide 100 per cent monitoring, or selective monitoring only, the finance required for any such system is considerable – especially if this has to be added to financial support for the CPD system itself. The burden will be particularly great for professions which have no governmental support, through such an agency as the NHS. Professions without such funding will have to find the necessary finance through members' fees (with possible supplementation through commercial sponsorship) and this is unlikely to be universally popular.

The ultimate fear is that, unless it can be shown that voluntary professional-led CPD is proving effective, compulsion may be introduced via legislation. There is little evidence that compulsion in the form of mandatory CPD would prove more effective (no profession has yet found it possible to strike off a member for failure to meet his or her CPD obligations) unless the legislation went so far as to require re-examination. However, on the evidence of the activities of the NCVQ, the professions do have cause to be anxious.

Our hopes
Our hopes for the future are largely based on the younger generation within the veterinary profession. Highly intelligent, responsive to their degree course education and training, and very keen to progress in their special field, the only question is whether they can be encouraged to maintain their interest and

enthusiasm as they progress through their professional careers. Can one make CPD an accepted way of life – which has not been the case for the majority of their predecessors?

Benefits accruing naturally from good CPD are greater expertise leading to greater client satisfaction and increased demand for one's services. In addition, and just as important, pursuing CPD in an area of special interest can lead to more interesting and less routine professional work, as well as feeling more comfortable and confident in what one is doing.

Once that is understood, support for the funding of CPD will follow, and those who have responsibility for promoting the programme must respond by ensuring considerable provision and choice, offered in attractive packages. One is advised that the United States is at least a decade ahead of the UK in such provision, and we can learn from the former in such areas as downtime television, which may be one field for inter-professional cooperation.

The Chartered Institute of Patent Agents

The Chartered Institute does not have a formal policy on CPD, nor really an informal one, although there is a guideline to the rules of professional conduct indicating that members should keep their knowledge and expertise up to date.

Hopes

There is a thirst for knowledge from patent agents evidenced by the success of conferences and training courses which are organized by or for the Institute. We hope therefore that members are undertaking CPD on this voluntary basis. The qualifying examinations for registration are based on practical knowledge acquired in training, but lack the skills-based competency testing which are becoming more common in other professional areas.

We are keen to promote awareness of patents and other forms of intellectual property in HEIs and are working to increase collaboration with university departments both to provide training to their undergraduates and to use their resources for training members in particular areas of the law.

Fears

In common with other professions, our fears revolve around the practicalities and expense of organizing a mandatory system of CPD, if such systems should be imposed by legislative action.

Small professions do not have the facilities to organize elaborate monitoring schemes, nor arrangements for accreditation of training providers or extensive self-provision of suitable CPD training courses.

Chartered Insurance Institute

For the Chartered Insurance Institute, CPD is a new concept; it was a condition which the Privy Council imposed in return for granting the widening of Chartered status within the profession to include all diploma-holders, not just Fellows. The driving force, therefore, for the introduction of the scheme did not come from within either the Institute or its membership.

However, the notion that learning should not stop with the completion of a professional qualification is gradually gaining support, although it is proving politically very difficult to agree the details of the scheme because the group of members at which it is aimed are the most senior group within the qualified membership and are, therefore, the most vocal.

The Institute has a role as an examining body and while it is strictly not a regulator, it polices the ethical behaviour of its membership. This has led to the CPD scheme being a sanctions model rather than a so-called benefits approach. One fear, therefore, is that compliance with CPD requirements will be seen as a chore and any training will not have any effect on ultimate performance.

Another fear is that because Chartered status within insurance is voluntary for diploma holders (and this is the target group for CPD) the scheme might flop, ie, people might simply decide to relinquish their Chartered status, retaining simply their post-nominal designatory letters which they have obtained by examination.

Another worry is that training organizations might not come forward to become accredited or – worse – large numbers of those affected might decide to be 'economical with the truth' when recording the training which they undergo.

On a more positive note our hopes are that the Chartered members will embrace the scheme wholeheartedly and behave in an adult fashion when recording the CPD. Flowing from this, it is to be hoped that the scheme will have a noticeable effect on the quality of the contribution which senior professionals within the industry can make to their employers' businesses.

A subsidiary benefit of the scheme which outsiders might regard as trifling but which we in the profession see as very important is the need to revitalize our local education provision. We hope that CPD will galvanize those responsible for education in the UK regions to provide far more effective training than they have been doing in the past. They will also need to provide training at a level which meets the needs of the Chartered membership, which by definition is not at an introductory or even an intermediate level.

In conclusion it is to be hoped that our CPD scheme, aimed as it is at the most professional group within the industry, will catalyse a more enlightened approach to education and training within the insurance and financial services industries. This will take many years to achieve and will require other initiatives (for example the development of NVQs throughout all levels), but CPD could be a step along this long road.

The Engineering Council

Hopes

All engineers will be committed to the need for adapting to change, and to continuous improvements to their performance as professionals. Continuous learning and CPD will be an integral part of this process

CPD will contribute positively to personal and business success; it will be a driving force for change relating to innovation and quality.

Professionals are individuals with unique learning needs and opportunities. However, there will be a focus on reviewing experience, seeking out learning opportunities, and planning/recording of learning achievements. A code of practice for CPD will provide a common agreed obligatory framework to underpin CPD, supported by professional engineering institutions.

Occupational standards will provide a necessary analytical method for identifying needs, planning action, and recording/reviewing achievements. It will be common language for individuals, employers and professional and academic institutions. It will enable a focus on outputs of CPD, rather than inputs.

There will be a greater use of a much wider range of CPD activities than courses. This will include peer group support (through mentoring, self-help groups, lunch time meetings) and a considerable increase in distance learning (use of TV, videos, etc.).

Activities will be based around regions and branches driving CPD for their members. There will be more collaboration between institutions and professions, particularly in joint activities in cross-disciplinary subjects.

Fears
CPD may increasingly be driven by administrative requirements of mandatory systems. This may take ownership away from the individual professional. People may do CPD because it is a requirement, rather than to improve their performance and career development.

Qualifications (whether these are educational, professional, or vocational) may become the driving force and benchmarks for CPD, thus detracting from measurements of the processes of learning and the achieved outputs in terms of competence and development.

Royal Institute of British Architects (RIBA)

RIBA *hopes* that:

- CPD will soon be at the heart of all of the Institute's activities;
- the CPD infrastructure of RIBA will be developed and improved;
- RIBA members will be further motivated and supported to manage their CPD and that practices will be encouraged to facilitate CPD;
- RIBA can educate the clients of architects in the importance of their architects' CPD;
- appropriate systems for monitoring and possibly rewarding CPD are implemented.

RIBA *fears* that these *hopes* may not come to fruition as rapidly as the Institute may wish, if the required resources for the implementation and maintenance of the CPD service are not available on a consistent basis.

Royal Pharmaceutical Society of Great Britain

The last five years have seen some major developments in the area of CPD, including:

- the development of an RPSGB strategy for continuing education and the implementation of some of its major recommendations;

- the establishment by the government health departments of national steering committees for pharmacy postgraduate education in England and Scotland (the Welsh Committee for Pharmacy Postgraduate Education has existed since 1979);
- the establishment in England of the Centre for Pharmacy Postgraduate Education funded by the Department of Health (with Section 63 funding), and similarly in Scotland, the Scottish Centre for Post Qualification Pharmaceutical Education;
- an increase in pharmacists undertaking postgraduate courses, particularly in clinical pharmacy;
- the development of professional audit.

Hopes for the next five years

- The introduction of a postgraduate education allowance, at least for community pharmacists, payable to the individual pharmacist on completion of a specified amount of continuing education. This system would obviously warrant some form of accreditation scheme, coupled with certificates of completion for participating pharmacists.
- The development of a formal means of recognition for pharmacists regulary participating in CE, such as certificates and/or postgraduate awards, possibly through a credit accumulation and transfer scheme (CATS).
- Continued support from the Department of Health and the other government health departments for the CPPE (England), SCPPE and the WCPPE.
- Continued support for the CPD planner and record (the first such planner was introduced in November 1993 with financial support from Glaxo Pharmaceuticals, UK Ltd).
- Secure funding for the adequate provision of continuing education opportunities for hospital pharmacists.
- The continued increased uptake by pharmacists of CE opportunities and a resulting increase in standards of service by the profession.

Fears

- A reduction in government support for CPD activities.
- The enforced introduction of audit/competence assessment from outside the profession.
- The introduction of postgraduate education allowance payments to pharmacy contractors from the existing global sum (ie, no new money or direct incentive).

- A reduction in the quality of provision by existing providers.
- Reduced uptake by pharmacists of government-funded cours-
  es, which could lead to withdrawal of some of the funding.
- Reduced uptake by pharmacists of any type of CE.

Index